What people are saying about

RED LETTERS

"Tom Davis is a man who lives the 'red letters' he talks about in this book. My family has traveled around the world with Tom and has seen firsthand the impact and effectiveness of his work. *Red Letters* is a must-read for every Christ-follower who wants to put the words of Jesus into practice—not just to relieve earthly suffering, but to reap eternal benefits."

—FRANK HARRISON, CHAIRMAN AND CEO,
COCA-COLA BOTTLING CO. CONSOLIDATED

"Tom Davis's book is an indictment against the complacent church, which has failed to be Jesus to the rejected and abandoned of the world, especially the millions of Africans suffering with HIV/AIDS. He makes the mind-numbing statistics come alive with the stories of individuals, and challenges Christians to be Jesus to them by giving tangible and realistic options for action."

—THE RIGHT REVEREND JOHN KABANGO RUCYAHANA,
BISHOP OF SHYIRA DIOCESE, EPISCOPAL CHURCH OF RWANDA

"You can't help but respond to Tom's passion."

—ROBERT C. ANDRINGA, PhD, PRESIDENT EMERITUS,
COUNCIL FOR CHRISTIAN COLLEGES & UNIVERSITIES

"I have known Tom Davis for many years. He is a man of integrity and a man of action. I can't think of a book that will inspire you and motivate you more than *Red Letters*."

—DR. JAMES L. GARLOW, BEST-SELLING AUTHOR, Cracking Da Vinci's Code,
SENIOR PASTOR, SKYLINE WESLEYAN CHURCH

"*Red Letters* challenges each of us to become Christlike—to show compassion and exhibit hope. Tom Davis offers both a biblical foundation and practical ways that we can be part of the solution to extreme poverty and preventable and treatable diseases."

—J. HAL BAILEY, EXECUTIVE VICE PRESIDENT, MARKETING AND OPERATIONS,
FAMILY CHRISTIAN STORES

"*Red Letters* is an inspirational call to action for a church that is in danger of missing God's call to care for the widow and the orphan. This is a book to be studied and shared amongst friends, family, and church members. It addresses one of the biggest gaps in Christianity today—the gap between Jesus' heart, broken for the poor, and our own still-calloused hearts.

—SETH BARNES, EXECUTIVE DIRECTOR AND FOUNDER, ADVENTURES IN MISSIONS

"Tom offers practical ways you can make a difference in the lives of millions around the world. May your heart bleed with compassion as you read, and may this book inspire you to step out and do what you can to impact others with the love of Christ."

—RON LUCE, PRESIDENT AND FOUNDER, TEEN MANIA MINISTRIES

"Tom Davis is an activist with a passion for the poor, the sick and the needy. Read this book and you will be captivated. Read this book and you will want to make a difference in the world. Tom combines a powerful motivational call with extremely practical suggestions to live a life of real faith in the midst of a hurting world."

—GARY WILKERSON, MINISTER, WORLD CHALLENGE

"HIV/AIDS is devastating our world, and the Christian church has been on the sidelines for too long. Tom Davis exhorts us to take the red-letter passages in the Bible seriously—to be Jesus to those who need Him, and let them be Jesus to us."

—E. BAILEY MARKS, DIRECTOR, CROSSROADS

"Tom's passion for the needy and the millions inflicted by the HIV/AIDS pandemic is contagious."

—DONALD H. WHITNEY, FOUNDER AND PRESIDENT, WORLD CHILDREN'S CENTER

"*Red Letters* offers a glimpse into the heart of God."

—PAUL PENNINGTON, DIRECTOR OF FAMILYLIFE HOPE FOR ORPHANS, A SUBSIDIARY OF CAMPUS CRUSADE FOR CHRIST

"Tom Davis is a prophetic voice that the church would do well to heed. He challenges us to be the hands and feet of Jesus to those who are suffering. This is a book for those who long to align their hearts' passion and their lives' work with the heart of God."

—ANDREW MCQUITTY, SENIOR PASTOR, IRVING BIBLE CHURCH

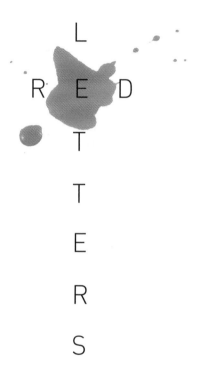

RED
LETTERS

TOM DAVIS

R E D
L
E
T
T
E
R
S

LIVING A FAITH THAT BLEEDS

David C Cook®

transforming lives together

RED LETTERS
Published by David C. Cook
4050 Lee Vance View
Colorado Springs, CO 80918 U.S.A.

David C. Cook Distribution Canada
55 Woodslee Avenue, Paris, Ontario, Canada N3L 3E5

David C. Cook U.K., Kingsway Communications
Eastbourne, East Sussex BN23 6NT, England

David C. Cook and the graphic circle C logo
are registered trademarks of Cook Communications Ministries.

The Web site addresses recommended throughout this book are offered as a resource to you.
These Web sites are not intended in any way to be or imply an endorsement on the part of
David C. Cook, nor do we vouch for their content.

Unless otherwise noted, all Scripture references are taken from *THE MESSAGE*. Copyright © by
Eugene H. Peterson 1993, 2002. Used by permission of NavPress Publishing Group. Scripture
quotations marked NIV taken from the *Holy Bible, New International Version*®. *NIV*®. Copyright ©
1973, 1978, 1984 International Bible Society. Used by permission of Zondervan. All rights
reserved; NASB are taken from the *New American Standard Bible*, © Copyright 1960, 1995 by The
Lockman Foundation. Used by permission; and NKJV are taken from the New King James
Version. Copyright © 1982 by Thomas Nelson, Inc. Used by permission. All rights reserved.

LCCN 2007904786
ISBN 978-0-7814-4535-1

Published in association with the literary agency of Alive Communications, Inc,
7680 Goddard St., Suite 200, Colorado Springs, CO 80920.

Cover Design: The DesignWorks Group, David Uttley
Interior Design: Karen Athen
Cover Photos: Phillip Parker; shutterstock

Printed in the United States of America
First Edition 2007

4 5 6 7 8 9 10

111009

To the almost fifty million people infected with HIV virus who are created in God's image, have value and purpose, and deserve to know they are loved and respected

CONTENTS

ACKNOWLEDGMENTS

I WOULD LIKE TO thank a few very special people for joining me on the journey and for making this book a reality.

Emily, my beautiful wife, who is more amazing than any man deserves.

Don Pape, my agent-gone-publisher. Thank you for believing in me and inspiring me.

Andrea Christian, for being so diligent in seeing this through. Thank you so much for your vision for this message.

Rick Christian and the folks at Alive Communications.

Matt Monberg, for helping me with creative ideas and being a great friend and colleague.

The staff at Children's HopeChest. We're in this together, and there's no group of people I'd rather work shoulder to shoulder with.

Steve Parolini, for the hours of labor helping me shape this book into what it has become.

Kari Miller, for the wonderful stories about the people and places in Africa.

Scott Todd, for providing information about HIV/AIDS.

Seth Barnes, Gary Black, and Andrew Shearman, for what's ahead.

INTRODUCTION

The Christian church owes an apology to the almost fifty million individuals in our world currently infected with HIV/AIDS.

Those of us who claim to follow Christ's teachings should be ashamed for what little we've done to help the countless millions of women, children, and orphans who have died or are dying. Entire nations are going up in flames while we watch them burn.

Bono and the supporters of the ONE Campaign are right to use words like "crisis" and "emergency" when talking about the situation in Africa. The continent is on fire with AIDS, and unless drastic action is taken, entire countries will be wiped off the face of the planet by this disease.

Sadly, the church has been slow to act in response to this crisis. Like the priest and Levite of Jesus' parable, we have passed by the man on the side of the road, too busy or too "holy" to involve ourselves in lending a helping hand.

Africa is indeed on fire. But as we argue or fuss about how it started and who should be saved first, thousands more children are orphaned each day. Every hour, another one thousand children will die. Did you know that you are just a short plane ride away from a world where eight-year-old girls prostitute themselves for food?

The true state of emergency lies within the church—it lies within us. It's *our* problem. We can't leave Africa's children lying by the side of the road as we pass on by.

HOPE

The gospel I believe in offers a cup of cold water in Jesus' name. The only gospel worth living is the one that incarnates love. The only gospel worth giving our lives for is the one that elevates the needs of others above our own. That's what the "good news" is all about.

And thankfully, there is more good news. Though the church has been slow to move, things are improving. National and local church leaders are beginning to challenge congregations to think globally when they offer that cup of cold water. Christian organizations are responding with more and more boldness. Still, we have a lot to learn and a long way to go. History will judge our generation by how we responded to those in need. History will judge the church by how it responded. We have an opportunity to show the world just what it truly means to be Christ-followers.

We *can* make a difference. We *can* change the world. When we lead with compassion, we can move from apology to action. And out of action springs hope—hope *and* life.

So, for our mistakes … I am sorry. But for our potential, for the impact you and I can have on a world in need … I am hopeful.

Tom Davis
cthomasdavis.com

Go and do the same.

—Luke 10:37

A LIVING GOSPEL

RUSSIANS CELEBRATE THE arrival of spring in March. During a Russian spring, temperatures hover just above freezing during the day, which melts the graying snow—only so it can freeze again into a world-covering sheet of ice at night. There are no tiny blooms reaching up through the earth to try to touch the sun. No patches of green to add color to the bleak landscape.

It was one of these spring nights when ten of us were walking down a dark, icy sidewalk in Vladimir. A young boy darted across the street, heading straight toward us. He was twelve, maybe thirteen, dirty and wearing tattered rags. He was speaking Russian. Asking for something. Pleading, perhaps.

"Sorry, we don't understand," we said. It was no lie.

But we did understand the voices inside our heads that spoke with equal measures of cynicism and sad resignation. Just another worthless beggar. If we gave him money, he'd probably spend it on drugs or cigarettes. If the kid really wanted help, there are plenty of shelters that could feed him and offer a place to sleep.

We kept walking. But something inside fought to quiet the voices. Something inside challenged me to act in a way consistent with the Savior I follow.

I turned, grabbed the translator by the arm, and went back after the boy. "Hey! Come back." *What do I say?* I thought. *Where do you begin to reach out to someone in need?* "What's your name?" I asked. "Kak tibya zavoot?" Dema, my translator, repeated in Russian. I got down on one knee so we were eye to eye.

"Kirill."

He was no longer just a beggar on the street. He was a little boy with a name—a name shared by a Russian Orthodox saint. I looked into his eyes. He had a story to tell. A story filled with pain and heartache. A story marked by hunger and homelessness. He was shivering. Somehow he'd survived the cold Russian nights.

Just a little boy.

"Hi, Kirill. My name is Tom. How can I help you?" Dema translated for me with a rapid-fire smorgasbord of Russian words.

Kirill had run away from a dangerous situation. He hadn't

eaten in three days. He looked so frail standing there. All he wanted was a place to stay and some food.

"Would you help me?" he asked.

That stupid voice went off in my head again. The same voice that speaks to me when I happen upon a panhandler back home in the States. *He'll probably just buy vodka if we give him money.* That inner voice—it's mine. And it very well could be speaking the truth. But it's not the voice I want to hear. I want to hear Jesus. Did he put conditions on the help he offered? A familiar story elbowed its way past my hesitancy. A story of Jesus helping a woman caught in adultery. Jesus didn't refuse to help the woman because she might sin again. He forgave her and told her to sin no more. She was worth the risk. She was worth helping.

"Kirill, here's money for food and a bus ride." We gave him the address to the ministry center for Children's HopeChest. There he would find help. We made arrangements for him and told the staff we would pay for whatever he needed.

Kirill took the money and walked off into the black night, fading into the distance like a ship on an uncertain journey.

I wondered what Jesus felt as he watched those he helped walk into the night. Did all of them live changed lives? Did they all stop sinning? Did they all hang on to the hope they had been missing?

About an hour later we received a phone call from the ministry center. Kirill had arrived and was receiving the care he needed. They would find him a place to live. Somewhere safe.

My cynical inner voice was silenced. I had only offered money for food and bus fare, but it was Jesus who had spoken to Kirill.

He didn't need a translator to hear Jesus' words now. Kirill was tasting them in a meal. Feeling their touch in the comfort of a warm blanket. And resting on them in the hope and promise of a good tomorrow.

He was just a little boy.

And on that cold spring night in Vladimir, Russia, he was Jesus.

You may be wondering, *Was that a typo? Didn't Tom mean that he, Tom, was Jesus to Kirill?* Of course we're called to be like Jesus. Colossians 3:10 (NIV) tells us to put on the new self, which is being renewed "in the image of its Creator." This is the basis of our spiritual formation, something Paul taught about with great passion and wisdom. And, yes, reaching out a helping hand to someone in need is one way we live out that Christlikeness.

But there is something else going on when we reach out to help the helpless—something unexpected. Something we often miss. Something that speaks not only to the process of becoming Christlike—to our spiritual formation—but also to the very truth of where we find Jesus.

LOOKING FOR JESUS

I've discovered a new way to live. Every morning when I get out of bed, I look for Jesus. No, not because I've misplaced him. And I'm not talking about a feeling I get during prayer, or revelation that comes to me while reading Scripture. I'm talking about finding Jesus in the eyes of real people. In the eyes of the poor, the handicapped, the oppressed, the orphan, the homeless, the AIDS victim—the abandoned and the forgotten.

Throughout Scripture, Jesus identified with the poor in amazing ways. He was their champion, their advocate. He gave them purpose and meaning and hope. He held them in high esteem and blessed them. There is something deep and meaningful about this. In Matthew 25:40, Jesus said, "Whenever you did one of these things to someone overlooked or ignored, that was me—you did it to me." Was he truly saying that we will find him in the lives of the poor? This is a rich mystery.

We shouldn't be surprised. Our God is indeed a God of mystery. Isaiah 55:8–9 says,

> "I don't think the way you think.
> The way you work isn't the way I work."
> God's Decree.
> "For as the sky soars high above earth,
> so the way I work surpasses the way you work,
> and the way I think is beyond the way you think."

You don't have to read very far into the New Testament before running head-on into one of the greatest of these mysteries. I don't know about you, but I (and more than a few Jews in Jesus' time) would have expected the King of the universe to be born in a palace—someplace worthy of his status. He would have slept on no less than four-hundred-thread-count Egyptian cotton crib sheets and rested his head on a down-filled, silk-wrapped pillow.

The mobile above his crib would surely have been crafted of sparkling gems—white diamonds, red rubies, blue sapphires, and green emeralds. And all of the most respected people in society would visit this beautifully decorated nursery to worship him.

But that's not how God did things. Jesus was born in a dirty, smelly, disgusting barn. He was laid not on a clean sheet but in a manger—a feeding trough filled with animal snot and drool and their leftover half-eaten food. He wasn't welcomed to the world by great leaders, by rulers and officials and other members of the Lexus-drivers club. He was met by a bunch of lowly shepherds. Yes, three kings or wise men arrived from the east months later. But nobody even knew who they were.

Are you getting the picture? Jesus didn't come to earth and identify with the rich, the successful, and the most influential. He entered the world as a pauper. He entered the world not in the comfort of his parents' home, nor in the company of smiling relatives or even the safety of a hospital. He arrived in the humblest of places, in the lowliest of circumstances. God hid the mystery of the kingdom in the lives of the most needy.

Is it any wonder, then, that Jesus associated himself with the "least of these"? That when we help them, we're helping Jesus? God has tremendous love for those who are rejected, abandoned, and laughed at. This truth came clear to me when I started reading about the life of Mother Teresa. Read what she said:

> The dying, the crippled, the mentally ill, the unwanted, the unloved—they *are Jesus in disguise*.... [Through the]

poor people I have an opportunity to be 24 hours a day
with Jesus. Every AIDS victim is Jesus in a pitiful disguise;
Jesus is in everyone.... [AIDS sufferers are] children of
God [who] have been created for greater things.[1]

In some crazy way, Jesus *is* the poor. When we find the "least
of these," we find him. If this doesn't turn your theology upside
down, I don't know what will.

There's a story told about an incredible transformation in an
old monastery because people lived out these truths. M. Scott Peck
recounted the story in his book *The Different Drum*.

The story takes place in an orthodox monastery in eastern
Europe, sometime in the early twentieth century. The monastery
was in danger of being shut down. For centuries it had been the
house of a great monastic order, but after hundreds of years of
persecution, and in an age when many people believed orthodoxy
was no longer relevant, the abbot and four monks found themselves to be the last members of the order. The branch houses
were long gone, and even in this one remaining location, the five
monks hadn't been successful in attracting new members. Each
of these monks was over the age of seventy. It didn't take a math-
ematical genius to see that the order was doomed. This caused
the monks a great deal of worry and anguish, but they remained
faithful: Every day they diligently, if sullenly, carried on their
work.

In the deep woods surrounding the monastery there was a little hut that a local rabbi occasionally used for retreat and

contemplation. One day it occurred to the abbot to ask the rabbi if he had any advice on how to save the monastery.

When the rabbi saw the abbot coming up the path, he went out to greet him. But when the abbot asked his question, the rabbi could only grieve with him. "I know how it is," he said. "The spirit has gone out of the people. It is the same in my town. Almost no one comes to the synagogue anymore." The old abbot and the old rabbi wept together. When the time came for the abbot to leave, they embraced each other.

"It has been a wonderful thing that we should meet after all these years," the abbot said, "but I have still failed in my purpose for coming here. Is there nothing you can tell me, no piece of advice that you can give me, that would help save my dying order?"

"No, I'm sorry," the rabbi responded. "I have no advice to give. The only thing I can tell you is that one of you is the Messiah."

When the abbot returned to the monastery, his fellow monks gathered around him to ask, "What did the rabbi say?"

"He couldn't help," the abbot answered. "We just wept and read the Torah together. He did say something as I was leaving— something cryptic: 'The Messiah is one of you.'"

In the days and weeks and months that followed, the monks pondered this and wondered whether there was any significance to the rabbi's words.

The Messiah is one of us? Could he possibly have meant one of us here at the monastery? Which one? Do you suppose he meant the abbot? Yes, if he meant anyone, he probably meant Father Abbot.

After all, he's been our leader for over twenty years. But if he meant Father Abbot, why didn't he say so? He might have meant Brother Thomas. Thomas is so gentle and kind; we all know that he's truly a holy man.

Certainly he didn't mean Brother David! David gets so crotchety. Then again, even though Brother David is a thorn in our flesh, he's nearly always right. Exceedingly right.

Well, the rabbi couldn't possibly have meant Aloysius. Aloysius is so passive, a real nobody. But he does have a gift for always being here when you need him. He just magically appears by your side. Maybe Aloysius is the Messiah.

Well, I know one thing for sure. The rabbi certainly didn't mean me. He couldn't possibly have meant me. I'm just an ordinary person. But what if he did? Suppose I am the Messiah? Oh God, I pray that it's not me. I wouldn't know how to be the Messiah.

As they contemplated in this manner, the monks began to treat each other with extraordinary respect on the off chance that one among them might be the Messiah. And on the off, off chance that each monk himself might be the Messiah, they began to treat themselves with extraordinary respect.

Because the forest in which it was situated was beautiful, people occasionally visited the monastery to picnic on its tiny lawn or to wander along some of its paths. As they did, without even being conscious of it, they sensed an aura of extraordinary respect that radiated from the monks and permeated the atmosphere surrounding the monastery. There was something strangely attractive, even compelling, about it. Hardly knowing why, people began to come back more frequently to picnic, to play, to pray. They brought friends to show them this special place. And their friends brought their friends.

Some of the younger folks who came to visit the monastery started talking with the monks. After a while, one asked if he could join them. Then another. And another. Within just a few years the monastery had become a thriving order and, thanks to the rabbi's cryptic gift, a vibrant center of light.

Does this story sound familiar? It should. Both the Old and the New Testaments tell similar stories—taking care of strangers, caring for those in need, and treating others like they could be angels in disguise.

LITTLE CHRISTS

You may be asking, "Well, what other way is there?" There have always been *two* ways. C. S. Lewis wrote, "The Church just exists to help people be little Christs." I certainly have met individuals and church families who live this out. But all too often, those of us who call ourselves Christians live in direct opposition to what Christ said we should do.

Living out the gospel is hard work. It's easy to talk about it. Any of us can sit in church and sing warm, happy worship songs that make us feel good. We can nod agreeably with the pastor's wisdom. And sometimes we can even drop a few extra dollars into the offering basket. But it's not so easy to actually go and *do* what Jesus said to do.

Jesus calls us to live in ways that go against our natural incli-
nations. For example, I don't have the easiest time living out this
verse: "I'm telling you to love your enemies. Let them bring out the
best in you, not the worst. When someone gives you a hard time,
respond with the energies of prayer, for then you are working out
of your true selves, your God-created selves" (Matt. 5:44–45).

Frankly, I want my enemies to burn. I want them to suffer for
the wrong they did to me. I want revenge. That's my initial
response. My human response. But because I have been redeemed
by Jesus' sacrifice, the truth of the living Christ who is ordering my
life challenges that response. I (sometimes slowly, often painfully)
embrace that truth and learn to say no to my human response and
yes to what Christ wants me to do.

Most of my life I have prayed that these sorts of transforma-
tions would occur almost magically. That I would wake up one day
and be a totally different person. That all of my desires would be
godly. That I would have a natural inclination to deny myself, pick
up my cross, and follow Jesus. That I would suddenly just love my
enemy. But it didn't happen like that.

Transformation *did* occur when I would hear the words of
Jesus and obey them, no matter how I felt. The more I obeyed, the
more I was transformed. I was becoming a different person because
I was *living* myself into it. I was becoming the words I saw on the
page. The words Jesus himself spoke.

What if all Christ-followers lived the Red Letter words in the
Bible—Jesus' words? What if we offered the hungry something to
eat, gave one of our many coats to someone who was cold, and

truly loved *all* our neighbors as ourselves? How radically different would our lives be? How different would our *world* be if Christians were really living as little Christs?

That's what this book is about. Learning to live a faith that is so real, you bleed Jesus. Here's how to start: Look for Jesus every morning in the eyes of the people you meet. And then look for him in the mirror.

"I desire compassion, and not sacrifice,"
for I did not come to call the
righteous, but sinners.

—Matthew 9:13 NASB

THIS
SHRINKING
WORLD

I WAS IN THE beautiful, mountainous region of Transylvania, Romania, when I learned beyond the shadow of a doubt that the world had changed. It was there, while on a mission trip in the land that was home to the real-life inspiration for Count Dracula—Vlad the Impaler—that my once-big world suddenly shrank.

Romania had recently become newsworthy not because of renewed interest in vampires but because of something even more evil—the horrible mistreatment of babies in orphanages.

Disturbing video footage of workers beating infants, throwing them around the room, and tying them to their cribs had made its way across the ocean, prompting immediate action from individuals and organizations intent on responding to this affront to humanity.

As we were driving along the countryside, I looked out of the bus window and watched the world float by as if in slow motion. Paintings of the idyllic agrarian lifestyle came to life before my eyes. Men standing in fields cutting hay as they swung sickles in time to some ancient rhythm. Women milking cows in their front yard, brushing away perspiration with the backs of their hands. Children tending vegetable gardens, dirt in their fingernails and delight in their eyes.

Then I saw him. A man walking on the road ahead of us. He was pulling an old wagon upon which was resting a large butter churn. I let my thoughts drift back to another time in America—one I've only read about. A time when life was both harder and simpler. A time when a butter churn wasn't a curiosity but a *necessary* piece of equipment and evidence of the long process required before anyone could enjoy a slice of buttered bread.

Just then we started to pass the man and his wagon. He was holding a hand to his ear. I squinted to see what ancient ritual he was practicing. What handed-down-over-the-ages tradition he was carrying on.

He was talking on a cell phone.

GLOBALIZATION

We live in a global society, one that has been—for better and worse—shrunken by technology. Whether it's a farmer talking on a cell phone or someone watching in horror as a news-feed from across the ocean shows infants being mistreated in Romania, this is not your grandparents' world.

Just how small is our world? The other day I called to make a hotel reservation for a trip I was making here in the States. The reservation agent I spoke to was in India. In less than ten hours I can be sitting in Moscow, Russia. We can have packages delivered overnight almost anywhere in the world. We can talk to anyone anywhere at almost any time. And we can know about anything that happens anywhere within seconds of its happening. Times have changed. We can't help but be impacted by the things that take place all over the world every day.

Thomas Friedman, a well-respected expert on the issue of globalization, has this to say about this new world order:

> Globalization is not just a phenomenon and not just a passing trend. It is the international system that replaced the Cold War system. Globalization is the integration of capital, technology, and information across national borders, in a way that is creating a single global market and, to some degree, a global village.
>
> You cannot understand the morning news or know where to invest your money or think about where the world

is going unless you understand this new system, which is influencing the domestic policies and international relations of virtually every country in the world today.[1]

In the past, what happened on the other side of the world didn't always concern us. *They* lived in their world, and *we* lived in ours. But everything has changed. Now what happens in Iraq or Russia or Africa happens as if in our own yards. We are global next-door neighbors. There is no more *they* and *we*.

We have to shift our old ways of thinking. We are global citizens, living in a connected world, governed by global principles. Either we realize this and accept it, or we will be swallowed by it.

The forward thinkers of our world accept this truth. Some exploit it to grow their businesses. Some wield it as a political weapon. Some use it to do good work. But what are we, as Christ-followers, to do with the truth of a shrinking world? This is important—critically important—for us to consider. After all, this world was God's before it was anybody else's.

When You Look at the World

U2 is one of the most well-known rock bands in the world. If you've watched the news any time in the past few years, you've probably run across stories featuring U2's lead singer, Bono—but these aren't stories about typical rock-star antics like smashing guitars or trashing hotel rooms. Bono's life was forever changed when he was challenged in the mid-1980s by Bob Geldof to feed the world. That summer he and his wife, Ali, visited Ethiopia. They spent much of their time in orphanages. One day he was approached by a man who held his son in his hands, begging Bono to take him. This man knew that in Africa his son would die, but in Bono's homeland, Ireland, he would live. Bono kindly refused the man, but that decision has haunted him ever since.

By his own admission, this event turned Bono into a "rock star with a cause." Today he is the most recognized advocate for relieving the worst troubles in Africa: extreme poverty and AIDS. He formed DATA (Debt AIDS Trade Africa) to help with the ever-evolving crisis. He asked Western nations to forgive the debt owed by the African nations so they could use the money to take care of the horrific problems of AIDS and starvation. He persuaded President Bush to pledge five billion dollars of aid to Africa over five years and then encouraged U.S. senators to push the proposed amount even higher—which they did.

Senator Jesse Helms and former Treasury Secretary Paul O'Neill credited Bono with showing them the connection between debt relief and fighting AIDS. Bono has been a bit of a prophet to many world leaders. But he is still dismayed that a nation such as America, which has the medical and financial resources to treat disease, has seemed unwilling to do something truly significant to combat AIDS in Africa—to take it on as a national challenge, like the rebuilding of Europe after World War II under the Marshall Plan. In an article in the *Boston Globe*, Bono challenged both political parties to place AIDS on their short list of convention issues:

We are the first generation that really can do something about the kind of "stupid" poverty that sees children dying of hunger in a world of plenty or mothers dying for lack of a 20-cent drug that we take for granted. We have the science, we have the resources, what we don't seem to have is the will. This is an opportunity to show what America stands for.

Antiretroviral drugs are great advertisements for American ingenuity and technology.

I love how he gets right to the heart of the issue. Bono has also suggested that American kindness could go a long way in preventing future acts of terrorism against the United States. Anti-American sentiment is on the rise around the world like at no other time in history. Acts of kindness toward others can make a significant impact on how the rest of the world views us. Through acts of kindness, we can help the world see us as people who care for the needs of others, advocates for the poor, defenders of orphans, and a people who rebuild and transform societies. Even aside from biblical obligations, Americans ought to have a national interest in being part of the solution. Bono continued,

Never before has this great country been so scrutinized, and never has the "idea" of America been under such attack. Brand USA could use some polishing, and I say that as a huge fan.... Eighteen million AIDS orphans by the end of the decade in Africa alone. What will they think of us, and from where will order be introduced into their chaotic lives? Whispering extremists attract recruits when hope has broken down. Surely, in nervous, dangerous times, it is smarter for America to make friends now of potential enemies than defend itself against them later.[2]

Bono doesn't have to do what he's doing. It is a choice. His rock-star success has earned him more money than he could spend in a lifetime and immense popularity, rivaling that of the Beatles. So why does he do it? Because he leads with his heart. To Bono, there is a deeper, spiritual meaning to our existence. He believes that *everyone* has the right to live.

A song on U2's CD All That You Can't Leave Behind speaks volumes about Bono's heart. It's called "When I Look at the World," and the lyrics talk about seeing the world through the eyes of someone else, someone who is able to truly see:

> I see an expression
> So clear and so true
> That it changes the atmosphere
> When you walk into the room
> So I try to be like you

Though I can't speak for Bono's intent in writing these lyrics, I see them as a beautiful picture of how Jesus looks at the world. This is a picture we, as Christ-followers, ought to study closely.

WHAT HAVE WE BECOME?

If we're not careful, we can be consumed by trying to protect what we have. Many of us have been tremendously blessed. Compared to those who live in poverty, Western and developed nations live in unbelievable abundance. Our poor would be considered rich in most countries in the world.

What do I mean by poverty?

Poverty is having very little food to eat.

Poverty is lack of shelter.

Poverty is being sick and not being able to see a doctor.

Poverty is not having access to school and not knowing how to read.

Poverty is losing a child to illness brought about by unclean water.

Poverty has many faces and none of them is pretty. Consider these difficult-to-comprehend facts: 1.2 billion people are estimated to live on less than one dollar per day, and almost 3 billion on less than two dollars per day.[3] Do the math: That's 3.9 billion of the 6.5 billion people who live in our world.[4] Doesn't it seem ridiculous to you that billions of people are living in poverty? With all our wealth, all our technology, and all our resources, why haven't we solved this problem? Almost 2.5 million children die every year because of malaria.[5] Hello? We have medicine that kills malaria. It's cheap. It's easy to transport. Yet, we aren't doing what it takes to get the medicine to the people who need it. Here's a surprising and disturbing truth about poverty that really ticks me off: It's *preventable*.

Even though we possess most of the wealth in the world, there are many who aren't doing anything to help the world's poor. I'm not talking about giving financially when we don't have money to give. I'm talking about giving out of our abundance.

Let's put this in perspective. I need to preface this by saying I love Starbucks coffee and I drink lots of it. But the four dollars I spend on a grande mocha with extra whip is enough to pay for the malaria medicine a child would need to stay alive in a third-world country. I don't say this to make anyone feel guilty. I am merely trying to illustrate how easy it is to save the life of one person.

Why don't we act? Why don't we choose to make a difference? One reason is because we're afraid. We spend most of our time trying to protect what we have, fearing what would happen if that went away. When we do this, we become shackled to our possessions. In essence, we limit our range of motion. We can't reach far enough to offer compassion because our arms are too busy holding all that we own. If, on the other hand, we recognize that what we have is a gift, then we can extend our reach. We discover that we can use a portion of our gift to improve someone else's life, maybe even to save someone else's life.

This is where the red letters glow bright. Jesus wants us to be all about doing good works like this. Obedience to God's command to reach out to those in need is a good enough reason to offer compassion through our actions. But there is another reason: These actions glorify God. In Matthew 5:16 (NASB), Jesus said, "Let your light shine before men in such a way that they may see your good works, and glorify your Father who is in heaven." Not only do we glorify God in an incredible way when we give compassionately, but we inspire others to do the same. What more of an invitation do we need?

So how does Jesus see the world? This question, more than anything else, should be our guiding principle in how we relate to the needs of the global community. Perhaps a good way to help us see how Jesus sees the world is to first examine how he *doesn't* see it. This parable written by Henry Nouwen paints just such a picture:

> Once there was a people who surveyed the resources of the world and said to each other: "How can we be sure that we will have enough in hard times? We want to survive whatever happens. Let us start collecting food, materials, and knowledge so that we are safe and secure when a crisis occurs." So they started hoarding, so much and so eagerly that other peoples protested and said: "You have much more than you need, while we don't have enough to survive. Give us part of your wealth!" But the fearful hoarders said: "No, no, we need to keep this in case of an emergency, in case things go bad for us, too, in case our lives are threatened." But the others said: "We are dying now, please give us food and materials

and knowledge to survive. We can't wait … we need it now!"

Then the fearful hoarders became ever more fearful since they became afraid that the poor and hungry would attack them. So they said to one another: "Let us build walls around our wealth so that no stranger can take it from us." They started erecting walls so high that they could not even see anymore whether there were enemies outside the walls or not! As their fear increased they told each other: "Our enemies have become so numerous that they may be able to tear down our walls. Our walls are not strong enough to keep them away. We need to put bombs on top of the walls so that nobody will dare to even come close to us." But instead of feeling safe and secure behind their armed walls they found themselves trapped in the prison they had built with their own fear. They even became afraid of their own bombs, wondering if they might harm themselves more than their enemy. And gradually they realized their fear of death had brought them closer to it.[6]

Building walls around our possessions and our lives leads to selfishness and hardened hearts. When we live with a "never enough" mentality, life is so overwhelming we couldn't possibly help someone else. Jesus didn't have a "never enough" mentality. He lived and breathed a "what can I offer?" mentality. It didn't matter where he was or what he was doing: He always took the time to help someone in need. It didn't matter if it was a prosti-tute, a tax collector, or someone who was demon possessed. Jesus always stopped what he was doing to help. As his people we are called to go and do the same.

Seeing the World Through the Eyes of Jesus

One word comes to me when I think of how Jesus lived his life: *compassion*. I love Matthew chapter 9. It begins with Jesus getting in a boat and crossing the sea. Some people hear that he is coming and load a paralytic friend on a first-century version of a gurney and rush him over to Jesus. Jesus not only heals the man but encourages him and forgives his sins.

Then Jesus decides to have lunch with a bunch of sinners and tax collectors. This is where he meets Matthew and calls him to be his disciple. The Pharisees are enraged by Jesus' actions. They can't believe he would have the audacity to eat with … with IRS agents and other … *sinners*. Of course they don't confront him; instead they gossip to his disciples. (Surely *you've* never done anything like this.) Jesus overhears them and says something brilliant that stops them in their tracks: "It is not those who are healthy who need a physician, but those who are sick. But go and learn what this means: 'I desire compassion, and not sacrifice,' for I did not come to call the righteous, but sinners" (Matt. 9:12–13 NASB).

The Pharisees thought they were doing everything right by obey-ing every jot and tittle of the law. But they had missed the point. It wasn't their sacrifice Jesus was concerned with. Jesus cared about how compassionate they were toward their neighbor. In this key Red Letter passage, Jesus defined his mission. He had come to the earth to help sinners—people who are struggling, people who are separated from God, people living in extreme poverty, the sick, the needy.

Soon after this missional revelation, Jesus raised a synagogue official's daughter from the dead, healed two blind men, and capped everything off by casting out demons from a man who was mute. Just another day in the life of our Savior. And then he continued through all of the cities and villages teaching, proclaiming the gospel of the kingdom, and healing many more people who were sick. I have to believe Jesus was totally exhausted after this. I know *I* would have been. I would have slipped away to the nearest bed and breakfast.

But not Jesus. Verse 36 (NASB) says, "Seeing the people, He felt compassion for them, because they were distressed and dispirited like sheep without a shepherd." Even after all that he had given, all that he had offered of himself to those in need, he was *still* overwhelmed with compassion. This was the driving force in his life. Jesus knew how special all people were. He knew they were created in God's image. He knew they had eternity marked in their hearts. He knew they were capable of so much more than what they were currently living for. And he knew they had a destiny to fulfill.

JESUS DIED FOR EVERYONE, RIGHT?

This leads us to an important and timely question. Whom did Jesus die on the cross to save? Okay, the obvious answer is sinners.

That would be all of us. But what does that mean, really? And how do we grasp the significance of that truth?

The Pharisees were constantly trying to justify their behavior. When Jesus said, "Love your neighbor as yourself," they responded with an accusatory question: "Who is my neighbor?" I find it interesting they didn't say something like, "Wow! That's really good teaching!" The Pharisees weren't really interested in Jesus' teaching. They were interested in promoting their own agenda. They didn't want to love the poor and the needy, and they certainly didn't want to help people who were considered "lower" than them. Jesus, knowing this, responded by telling them the parable of the good Samaritan. (Samaritans were half-breeds—a people reviled by the Jews and certainly by Jewish leaders like the Pharisees.) The parable of the good Samaritan would have hit the Pharisees right where it hurt most—their pride. If they wanted to follow the teachings of Jesus, they would have to love the dirty Samaritans as much as they loved themselves. Not such an easy task for a people who believed (quite accurately, though it blinded them from a greater truth Jesus himself was teaching) that they were God's special people, God's chosen.

I know you've heard this verse a million times. Heck, if you've ever attended Sunday school, or for that matter watched a football game on television, you probably have it memorized. John 3:16 (NASB) states, "For God so loved the world, that He gave His only begotten Son, that whoever believes in Him shall not perish, but have eternal life." Could the verse be any clearer? Jesus wasn't sent to die for a person or one particular nation. He came to die for the *world*, the whole world.

Yeah, everyone. Jesus came to die for the terrorist who wants to blow up the building where you work. He came to die for Osama bin Laden. He came to die for the pervert, the child molester, and the convicted rapist. Intellectually, this makes sense. Of *course* Jesus came to die for all sinners. However, sometimes it can be a difficult truth to wrap your heart around.

Consider Jesus' last act of compassion before breathing his final breath: He forgave a thief who was dying on the cross next to him. This was not a wrongly convicted man of high standing but a dirty, rotten, rightly convicted thief. I suspect the man lived a horrible life. Certainly he didn't deserve to be forgiven. And, of course, that's the crux of the gospel message. *I* don't deserve to be forgiven either. None of us deserves forgiveness, but God offers it anyway. Not just to some, but to all.

We are created by a God who loves his creation. *All* of his creation. He wants all of us to know him and follow him. There are no geographical limits to God's love. God loves me just as much as he loves the little African baby I met who was about to die from tuberculosis she got because of the AIDS virus. This little baby was created in God's image just like I was. There is no difference between us in God's eyes. But there is *one* difference in my eyes— one that compels me to reconsider my abundance and the manner in which I view the world around me: She was born in Africa. An Africa where poverty and disease and death are infinitely more ubiquitous than Starbucks.

And, according to Jesus' parable, she is my neighbor. Yours, too.

I want to level the playing field. Something's gone wrong in the world that God created. There are a million little reasons why (and one big one—sin), but at the end of the day I'm left with the responsibility to do something. To reach out with compassion to the neighbor across the street *and* the neighbor across the ocean. When through a little effort or a lot of effort, I help save the lives of people who are less fortunate, I begin to see the world as God does. I begin to live out Jesus' Red Letter command to love my neighbor as I love myself.

Many playing fields around the world are in need of leveling. But one in particular is crying out louder than the rest. An entire civilization is being burned to the ground before our eyes.

See that you do not look down on one of these little ones. For I tell you that their angels in heaven always see the face of my Father in heaven.

What do you think? If a man owns a hundred sheep, and one of them wanders away, will he not leave the ninety-nine on the hills and go to look for the one that wandered off? And if he finds it, I tell you the truth, he is happier about that one sheep than about the ninety-nine that did not wander off. In the same way your Father in heaven is not willing that any of these little ones should be lost.

—Matthew 18:10–14 NIV

THE
CRADLE OF
CIVILIZATION

ONE OF MY earliest impressions of Africa was formed when I was a kid in Sunday school. My fourth-grade Sunday school teacher was a nice enough man, but like any memorable Sunday school teacher, he had his moments. Moments prompted, most likely, by unruly fourth graders like me. In those moments, his glasses would slide down low on his nose, he would crinkle his forehead (giving purpose to well-earned wrinkles) and say with far too much passion, "If you are a disobedient child, God may send you to Africa as a missionary!" Immediately, my lips and tongue went dry as I pictured the place where the worm doesn't die and the fire isn't quenched. I tried to imagine a fate slightly less frightening—like being sent to teach fourth graders in Sunday school. But despite my efforts to change the channel, images of skeletons in the sand—skeletons still grasping dusty Bibles—were seared into my young brain. My prayer life was strong, if solitary in purpose, during that season of life.

"God, I'll obey. Please don't send me to Africa!"

I would have been amazed then to discover that Africa is a place of exquisite beauty. Sure, Africa has its share of deserts, including the desert to beat all deserts: the Sahara. But Africa is also filled with lush rolling hills. With majestic mountains, verdant valleys, and endless plains, it is a place of incredible diversity. A land teeming with life. The home of lions, elephants, leopards, water buffalo, and rhinos. The playground of giraffes, crocodiles, and zebras.

Africa is exotic, magical, beautiful, and ancient. It is home to some of the most incredible civilizations in the world, including the Egyptians and the Ethiopians. It is a land overflowing with mystery, from the wonder of the pyramids to the riches of King Tut to the lure of the winding Nile River flowing down through Sudan to countries like Rwanda, Tanzania, and Uganda.

It is sometimes easy to forget that Africa played significant geographical roles in our biblical history. Mary and Joseph collected their baby Jesus and fled to Africa from the persecution of Herod. Joseph of the Old Testament was sold into slavery and taken to Egypt. The children of Israel served as slaves in Egypt. Moses married an Ethiopian woman. The list goes on.

Africa is an old continent. An ancient place with more history than can be recorded in a social studies textbook or a thousand Wikipedia entries. George Abungu, director-general of the National Museums of Kenya, said, "So far the evidence that we have in the world points to Africa as the Cradle of Humankind."[1]

Many believe that Africa contained the very first signs of human existence. A number of respected biblical archaeologists place the location of the garden of Eden in Africa—somewhere east of the Nile River in the area known today as Al Mansura in Egypt. Could it be true?

Even scientists are asking, "Is this where humans originated?" One of the oldest fossils unearthed was discovered in Ethiopia, in an area known as the Afar Depression. Perhaps you've read about this find—she goes by the name of "Lucy" and has been featured in *National Geographic* and *Time* magazines. Lucy is important to science because she is considered to be humankind's earliest known ancestor.

SHADOWS ACROSS THE LAND

Tales of the hunt, as told by the hunter, never glorify the lion.

—AFRICAN PROVERB

Fair-skinned westerners weren't a welcome sight to Africans. Consider this early impression taken from a Zulu epic poem,

Emperor Shaka the Great (trans. Mazisi Kunene), which draws on the memories of multiple Zulu oral historians: "They resemble us, but in appearance are the color of pumpkin-porridge.... They are rude of manners and without any graces or refinement. They carry a long stick of fire. With this they kill and loot from many nations."

With all of the glories Africa has to offer, it is also the birthplace of many sad stories. The transatlantic slave trade, centered in Africa, was one of the ugliest chapters in world history and left a permanent stain on the whole world. Of course, the people and the economies in Africa paid the greatest price for this tragedy. It has been estimated that more than fifteen million Africans were forcibly taken out of their homes and sold as slaves.

How was it possible that such a terrible trafficking of human cargo was allowed to go unchecked for more than four hundred years before the heartstrings of humanity were tugged in sympathy to say, "Enough!" There are several reasons, and you're probably not going to like any of them.

THE CHURCH DID WHAT?

Amazingly, the slave trade grew with the active support of both church and state, the primary powers that ruled Europe. The imperial visions of Henry the Navigator (son of John I of Portugal), Henry VIII, Elizabeth I, Charles II, and Isabella and Ferdinand of Spain focused on exploration, discovery, and dominion. Each "new" territory that was discovered was claimed by the explorer for his monarch. East and west, the Indies and the Americas, European expansion and conquest fulfilled the grandiose dreams of its blood-related royal families.

Worse still, the trade was rubber-stamped by Christianity. A succession of popes supported Portuguese and Spanish atrocities in the Americas in the sixteenth century. The indigenous peoples of the islands and the Africans imported into the colonies were considered savages by Europeans—savages who needed to be brought to the light of Christianity. The church simply overlooked what was happening to these Africans in the name of commerce and expansion and misappropriated evangelical intent.

ALL MEN ARE CREATED EQUAL?

Africans were caricatured as dark savages from a dark continent. Many people believed Africans were an inferior race. Some even believed that inferiority stemmed from the biblical curse on the children of Ham, who would forever be "hewers of wood and drawers of water." You may remember Ham as the man who looked upon the nakedness of his father, Noah, and was cursed by God.

This sort of thinking made it easy for non-Africans to convince themselves that slavery was simply an African's destiny. Scientific evidence would later be manipulated to justify these claims, classifying Africans as "sub-human" as an excuse for the excesses of the slave trade. One terrible result of this demonic philosophy was a sort of "programming" or conditioning of the European mind-set that became the very foundation of racism. Despite the "all men are created equal" truth preached by so many people in the decades that followed, most notably Martin Luther King, Jr., echoes and ripples of that mistaken mind-set still affect us today.

MONEY

When imperial powers began to take over Africa, a new chapter began. But it was not a better chapter. This chapter was all about expansionism and the rivalry between British and German imperial powers. Greed for the wealth of newly discovered diamonds and gold fueled the raging spirit of colonialism that would decimate the continent.

Greed became the driving force behind the slave trade. Greed was also responsible for the removal of Africa's resources. There was no concern for what these actions would do to the people or how they would strip the country of means to sustain their economy. There was nothing fair about it. It was a different kind of terrorism, an economic terrorism that proved the biblical truth: "The love of money is the root of all evil."

Even today Africa still suffers from this curse. Though billions of dollars have been poured into the continent to help undo the injustice that has been done, Africa is poorer today than ever. Why? Because much of Africa has not been taught how to develop a sustainable economy. Money is poured into crops like tea and cotton so foreigners can make money, but Africans can't eat tea and cotton. The crops they need to cultivate in order to survive are ignored. Because of this, millions starve.

These kinds of practices have set the stage for some of the world's most horrendous atrocities.

Genocide

The term *genocide* was coined in 1943 by Jewish-Polish lawyer Raphael Lemkin, who combined the Greek word *genos* (race or tribe) with the Latin word *cide* (to kill). The international legal definition of the crime of genocide is found in Articles 2 and 3 of the 1948 Convention on the Prevention and Punishment of the Crime of Genocide.

Article 2 of the convention defines *genocide* as any of the following acts committed with the intent to destroy, in whole or in part, a national, ethnic, racial, or religious group, such as

- Killing members of the group;
- Causing serious bodily or mental harm to members of the group;
- Deliberately inflicting on the group conditions of life calculated to bring about its physical destruction in whole or in part;
- Imposing measures intended to prevent births within the group;
- Forcibly transferring children of the group to another group.

In short, genocide is the systematic killing of an entire group of people. This is exactly what Hitler attempted to do with the

Jewish people. This terrible evil has surfaced in multiple African nations. Africa has had more occurrences of genocide than any other place in the world.

Many in our generation are aware of the terrible crisis that struck Rwanda in 1994. An estimated 800,000 Tutsis and moderate Hutus died in the genocide. These precious people—men, women, and children—were hacked to death with machetes while the rest of the world watched. More than anything, apathy in the hearts of the people of the world allowed this to occur. If we would have acted on our compassion, if we would have made our voices heard, this could have been prevented. At the very heart of this book is my desire to make our voices heard. To act out of compassion and then watch as our actions do make a difference.

As you read this book, genocide continues in Sudan. On Friday, September 10, 2004, in *The Washington Post*, Secretary of State Colin Powell said for the first time that genocide was taking place in Sudan and that both the government in Khartoum and government-sponsored Arab militias known as Janjaweed bore responsibility for rapes, killings, and other abuses that left 1.2 million black Africans homeless. Today, because we have been frozen voyeurs, an estimated 400,000 people have been systematically slaughtered, and over 2.5 million have been displaced.

The Second Congo War began in 1998 and "officially" ended in 2003 when a transitional government took power. This has been the widest interstate war in modern African history, directly involving nine African nations, as well as twenty armed groups. It has been called "Africa's World War" and the "Great War of Africa." An estimated 3.8 million people have died, mostly from starvation and disease brought about by one of the deadliest conflicts since World War II.

But the war didn't end in 2003. In 2004, more than one thousand people were dying from this genocide every single day. And so it continues. But unbelievably there is something even more deadly than this conflict.

HIV/AIDS

The HIV/AIDS crisis threatens the life not only of millions of Africans but also the rest of the world. The disease is spreading so fast that by the time you read these statistics, they will be horribly outdated.

Africa is considered the birthplace of this modern-day plague. In 1959, a plasma sample taken from an adult male living in what is now the Democratic Republic of Congo became evidence of the earliest known HIV infection.[2]

So what exactly does HIV/AIDS do? AIDS is caused by the human immunodeficiency virus (HIV), which progressively destroys the body's ability to fight infections and certain cancers. AIDS stands for acquired immunodeficiency syndrome.

- Acquired means that the disease is not hereditary but develops after birth from contact with a disease-causing agent (in this case, HIV).

- Immunodeficiency means that the disease is characterized by a weakening of the immune system.
- Syndrome refers to a group of symptoms that collectively indicate or characterize a disease. In the case of AIDS, this can include the development of certain infections and/or cancers, as well as a decrease in the number of certain cells in a person's immune system.[3]

During 2005, some 4.1 million people became infected with the human immunodeficiency virus. The year also saw 2.8 million deaths from AIDS—a record global total, despite antiretroviral (ARV) therapy, which reduced AIDS-related deaths among those who received it.[4]

Approximately half of the people who acquire HIV become infected before they turn twenty-five and typically die of the life-threatening illness called AIDS before their thirty-fifth birthday. By the end of 2005, the epidemic had left behind 15.2 million AIDS orphans, defined as those under eighteen who have lost one or both parents to AIDS.

The worst thing about HIV/AIDS is how it destroys the lives of its innocent victims. I'm talking about babies who are born HIV positive, little girls who are raped by their uncles and fathers, and even the women who are infected by the disease because their unfaithful husbands brought it home to their marriage beds. These victims are dying by the hundreds of thousands. But numbers like this can be overwhelming. Incomprehensible. Let me bring it down to earth for you.

WHY WE NEED TO HELP

A happy baby boy is bouncing in a crib in southern Africa. He looks and acts just like any other baby you've seen. He coos, laughs. There is a spark of genuine joy in his bright eyes. Turn your head just a bit. Look over there—in the corner of the room. Do you see that woman with the lifeless eyes? She is the baby's mother. She looks down when you catch her eye, and though she knows you mean her no harm, you can sense the fear marked by her bowed head.

You want to know her story, so you ask questions. It is difficult to ask—what do you say? But it is even more difficult to hear her answers. She is the victim of an AIDS cleansing ritual. The victim of a lie. It is a lie that circulates across Africa and states that if you have sex with a virgin you will be cured of AIDS. This beautiful woman was systematically raped by men who thought her virgin blood would cure them.

And that bouncing boy? That smiling baby? He was the product of that gang rape. His mother is dying of AIDS. And someday, a day that could steal the joy from this boy's eyes, he will learn that he is infected by HIV.

Sadly, this story is not unique. The number of people who are infected with HIV, through no fault of their own, is staggering:

In 2005, several hundred thousand children aged 14 or younger became infected with HIV. Over 90% of newly infected children are babies born to HIV-positive women, who acquire the virus at birth or through their mother's breast milk. Almost nine-tenths of these transmissions occur in sub-Saharan Africa. Africa's lead in mother-to-child transmission of HIV is firmer than ever despite the evidence that HIV ultimately impairs women's fertility; once infected, a woman can be expected to bear 20% fewer children than she otherwise would. Drugs are available to minimize the dangers of mother-to-child HIV transmission, but these are still often not reaching the places where they are most needed.[5]

PREVENTION AND EDUCATION

There is some good news. The good news is that most of these HIV infections can be prevented in ways that are cost effective and easy to implement. So why, then, does the disease continue to spread? That's the bad news: Ignorance persists in third-world countries about how HIV is spread.

There is significant tension in South Africa concerning the methods used by different medical practices to treat HIV. As many as 80 percent of people living in African countries seek healing through traditional African healers and use traditional African remedies.[6] Some of these traditional treatment methods are potentially harmful to people living with HIV—especially those people who are also taking more modern medicines. Consider this example. Some health experts, including the African health minister, claim that the African potato boosts the immune system and thereby helps to fight AIDS. However, a recent study shows that people taking ARVs should *not* eat African potato, because it lowers the level of antiretroviral chemicals in the body and increases the likelihood of HIV developing resistance to the drugs.[7]

This kind of misinformation just propagates the disease. Proper educational tools are needed to help understand how HIV is really spread. You've heard the statement "an ounce of prevention is worth a pound of cure"? This couldn't be truer in regard to this disease.

The missing piece? The missing piece is us. Yes, this problem is massive. In the next chapter, you'll begin to see just how massive. But when good people mobilize, they can make a massive difference in the lives of others. One at a time, we need to stand up. We need to open our eyes wide to the AIDS crisis in Africa.

I am the world's Light.

—John 8:12

4

PANDEMIC

EPIDEMIC IS AN UGLY, scary, and deadly word. It's the word we use to describe a disease that spreads rapidly in a community or over a large geographical area and causes thousands upon thousands of deaths. It's the word we've used for years now to describe the HIV/AIDS crisis. But if you've been watching the news lately, you've probably noticed a different (though similar) word is now being used to describe the crisis. The news media knows as well as anyone the power of "naming" things. Words have the power to give something significance. And what is the new word being bandied about? *Pandemic.* Yeah, sounds a lot like epidemic, doesn't it? Only bigger. And that's essentially what it means. A pandemic is an epidemic over a wide geographic area that affects a large proportion of the population.[1] It's a mega-epidemic.

You can fault the news media for exploiting words as mere commodities if you like, but with this one they've got it exactly right. The HIV/AIDS crisis is indeed a pandemic. It has crossed border after border and shows no signs of slowing down. And no place in the world is being hit harder by this pandemic than the continent of Africa. Though the region is home to just over 10 percent of the world's population, it contains more than 60 percent of all people living with HIV. An estimated 2.8 million adults and children became infected with HIV during 2006. This brought the total number of people living with HIV/AIDS in the region to 24.7 million.[2]

THE PREVALENCE OF AIDS AROUND THE WORLD

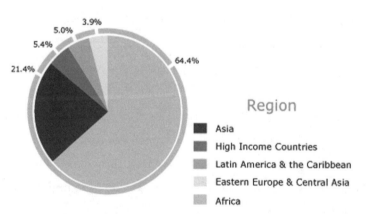

But back to that word—*pandemic*. It's a big word for a big problem. It gives us a name for something too big to name. In some ways, it's meaningless. Impersonal. But a pandemic isn't merely a function of mathematics, of statistics. It is the accumulation of millions of little stories. Stories of real people living real, pain-filled lives. And each story is a nightmare.

KISUMU

Located on the shores of Lake Victoria, Kisumu is the largest town in western Kenya. For many years, Kisumu was well known for its beauty and its unrivaled fishing industry. It was a refuge for hundreds of bird species, rich vegetation, and a thriving population. People would travel for miles to visit Hippo Point just to experience the exquisite and rare splendor of watching the sun set on Lake Victoria. Families and communities flourished along the banks of the lake. They were a happy people. A joyful people. But all of that is gone.

The land is decaying. The lake is drying up. The grasslands are disappearing.

And so are the people. One in three adults in Kisumu has HIV.

If you toured this city, you would find palpable evidence of what a pandemic does to a people. You would find abandoned villages—not because the people left for greener pastures, but because everyone is dead. Kisumu is a mere skeleton of what it used to be. It is an eerie, empty place. Where once the sounds of vivacious children playing and laughing filled the air, only fading echoes remain. Communities have disintegrated. Trade and industry suffer for lack of workers. Celebrations have given way to funerals. Life to death.

Hope is hard to find in Kisumu. Just ask Happiness, a member of the community. This is her story told in her own words.

My name is Happiness. I am now thirteen years old. I was born in Kisumu City, next to the shores of Lake Victoria. I remember my early days when I would swim and fish in the dark blue waters of Lake Victoria. Sometimes I thought that the lake was the biggest gift that Mother Nature has given to the people of western Kenya and East Africa as a whole.

My papa was a fisherman, and Mama would wait for the fishermen to come back in the morning from an all-night fishing trip, and she would get the fish and rush to the market. I watched and participated in this with great joy. In western Kenya standards, I would say my papa was a rich man. We could afford new clothes every Christmas and school fee and three square meals in a day. I knew there were poor people around us. Some neighbors could come to borrow salt, money, and food from my mama. She was kind. She always gave cheerfully.

Then suddenly, Papa was no longer going to work. He spent his days in bed in the house. Mama was the only one working. Papa grew thinner and thinner. Mama worked harder and harder. Papa passed away after a long battle with sickness. By that time Mama was also very ill. In Africa we believe nobody dies without a reason. People said it was my papa's business rivals who had bewitched him.

As if that was not enough, Mama also fell sick and died. It was the saddest day of my life—both my parents dead in a span of six months. I was only six years old.

That was many years ago. But the pain still lingers. I still hate death. I thought I was the only one who hates death in my village, but I'm not. We all fear death because it robs us. In East Africa, many of us are orphans as a result of the death of our parents. When death strikes, we feel it more than anyone, for we know what it has done to all of us.

This Christmas, I will not be getting a gift from my mama or papa. They are so silent in the grave. Before they went away, I was sure of Christmas gifts and three meals in a day, new clothes, respect, and love. Today, I am just another statistic. They call us African orphans, orphaned as a result of AIDS.

Death is a criminal. Whether it comes through a road accident or a sickness, it is a robber. To us in Kenya, we will never forgive death for taking away our parents and loved ones.

A story like Happiness's is difficult to hear. But if hers were the only sad story, there would be no need for this book. It would be easy to help one person in need. But what do we do when the needs are a million times greater?

THE POWER OF A PANDEMIC

To understand the magnitude of what we are facing with the HIV crisis, we have to go back quite a few years—to the 1330s. It was during this time that the world faced its most serious pandemic because of the bubonic plague.

It started as an outbreak in China and spread quickly across the modern world. The bubonic plague mainly affected rodents, but fleas transmitted the disease to people, which made it proliferate rapidly. Of course, at the time, nobody was sure how the disease was spreading, so naturally, they didn't know how to prevent it. Once people were infected, they would infect others. The plague caused fever and a painful swelling of the lymph glands (called "buboes," which is how the plague got its name) and also caused spots on the skin that were red at first before turning black. This gave the plague its other name: the "black death."

An eyewitness told what happened:

> Realizing what a deadly disaster had come to them, the
> people quickly drove the Italians from their city. But the
> disease remained, and soon death was everywhere. Fathers
> abandoned their sick sons. Lawyers refused to come and
> make out wills for the dying. Friars and nuns were left to

care for the sick, and monasteries and convents were soon deserted, as they were stricken, too. Bodies were left in empty houses, and there was no one to give them a Christian burial.[3]

The disease struck and killed people with terrible speed. The Italian writer Giovanni Boccaccio (1313–1375) said its victims often "ate lunch with their friends and dinner with their ancestors in paradise."[4]

By the following August, the plague had spread as far north as England. A terrible killer was loose across Europe, and medieval medicine was no match for it.

In winter the disease seemed to disappear, but only because fleas are dormant in winter. Each spring, the plague attacked again, killing new victims. After five years, twenty-five million people were dead—one-third of Europe's people.

Medieval society never recovered from the results of the plague. So many people had died that there were serious labor shortages all over Europe. The very idea of family was eradicated, and people lived in fear of dying every single day.

Is This a Fair Comparison?

Perhaps you're already questioning my comparison of the plague to the HIV/AIDS crisis. You should. They are very different in many ways. Fleas don't carry HIV. People don't pass it along through casual contact. For these reasons alone, HIV doesn't strike with the speed of the plague. If it did, hundreds of millions of people would die every year. However, I am making this comparison because there is much we can learn from the impact of the plague—much that should not only grab our attention but also move us to action.

Both the plague and the HIV/AIDS crisis have killed millions of people. The plague wiped out one-third of Europe's population. Many African nations are facing the same type of elimination, just over a longer period of time. Swaziland had an HIV infection rate at the end of 2004 of 42.6 percent. Faith Dlamini, the national coordinator of AIDS prevention with the National Emergency Response Council on HIV/AIDS, expressed her feelings about the situation: "There is hopelessness; what we are doing is not working."[5]

Unless something is done, half of Swaziland's population will be wiped off the face of the earth. When you walk around the streets of Mbabne, the capital city, and in the villages, you immediately notice an absence of young to middle-age adults. It's like the rapture has hit, but it's a rapture of a different kind—a dark, evil rapture. Soon, Swaziland will be a nation of orphaned children.

Or consider South Africa, one of the continent's largest countries with a population of over forty-four million people. Almost one-third of the people living there are infected with HIV. It's hard to fathom that more than fourteen million people will be dead in five to seven years if nothing is done to help them. And that number will continue to climb.

Estimated HIV prevalence among antenatal clinic attendees, by province in South Africa[6]

Province	2000 prevalence %	2001 prevalence %	2002 prevalence %	2003 prevalence %	2004 prevalence %	2005 prevalence %
KwaZulu-Natal	36.2	33.5	36.5	37.5	40.7	39.1
Mpumalanga	29.7	29.2	28.6	32.6	30.8	34.8
Gauteng	29.4	29.8	31.6	29.6	33.1	32.4
North West	22.9	25.2	26.2	29.9	26.7	31.8
Free State	27.9	30.1	28.8	30.1	29.5	30.3
Eastern Cape	20.2	21.7	23.6	27.1	28.0	29.5
Limpopo	13.2	14.5	15.6	17.5	19.3	21.5
Northern Cape	11.2	15.9	15.1	16.7	17.6	18.5
Western Cape	8.7	8.6	12.4	13.1	15.4	15.7
National	24.5	24.8	26.5	27.9	29.5	30.2

These events are not isolated to just a few of the countries in Africa; the disease is spread throughout the entire continent. Zimbabwe is a prime example. Early in 2003, over a third of the adult population was infected with HIV. It is estimated that at least one in three of today's fifteen-year-olds in Zimbabwe will die from AIDS. James T. Morris, executive director of the World Food Program, stood before the U.S. House of Representatives House Committee on Foreign Affairs deeply concerned about that country and the number of people who were on the brink of starvation. AIDS was fueling the problem to levels never before seen. He said, "This is the first major food crisis in history in which we clearly see that AIDS is playing a major role."[7]

Over a million children in Zimbabwe have lost one or both of their parents to AIDS. Because they are faced with extreme poverty and nothing to eat, they follow what they believe to be the only courses that offer any hope of survival. They become thieves. They fall prey to alcohol abuse. And when things get really bad (which is far too often), they join gangs or become pimps. They become soldiers, children schooled in the act of killing. Many of the young girls sell their bodies to survive. Some do it for food, others for money. They embrace the risk (which is almost a certainty) of becoming infected with HIV in exchange for a loaf of bread. I don't need to tell you it isn't a fair trade.

THE PERFECT STORM

In many ways, the HIV/AIDS crisis is far more devious than the plague. It certainly is more complex. Whereas the plague was eventually cured through vaccination, stemming the tidal wave of HIV requires a multifaceted approach because the proliferation of the disease is due to a multitude of factors, such as:

- Poor nutrition, bad general health, and therefore a weakened immune system (which allows the virus to more easily gain hold);
- Lack of knowledge concerning HIV and treatment options among the African people;
- Sexual behaviors among youth—70 percent of children not in school are actively engaged in sexual behavior.[8]
- Poverty—in order to survive, women are forced into transactional sex;

- Cultural norms regarding women—women have no rights over their own lives or bodies; if a man wants to have sex with her, she is unable to say no.

The disease itself also has unique properties that exacerbate the problem. When HIV is in the company of other diseases, it suddenly becomes even more deadly. HIV works completely differently from a bacteria or a virus. It actually works to destroy the immune system by copying a person's DNA in such a way that the CD4+ cells, the cells that control the immune system, don't work anymore. It makes a copy of its own DNA and hides it in the cell among your normal DNA. When the body is attacked by a disease, the cell starts to multiply and spreads the HIV all over the body.

So when a disease like malaria is present and the body does what it is supposed to do by defending itself, the HIV virus "wakes up." As the cells are dividing to defend the body, the HIV is destroying it. When a person infected with HIV also gets infected with the malaria parasite, the amount of HIV in the blood shoots up sevenfold.[9]

THE IMPACT

Although the end result—death—is always the same, HIV ravages societies in many different ways.

It wipes out worker populations. What would happen in the United States if the majority of our workforce was either dead or too sick to report for work?

Who would manufacture our cars?

Where would we find our health-care workers and civil leaders for our governments?

Who would work at our water treatment plants, grocery stores, and restaurants?

Where would we find teachers for our kids?

Where would our children find wives and husbands?

This is exactly what people in Africa are facing. There are few educators to teach the next generation because many of them have died. As a result, in some areas, school fees have gone up over 1,000 percent![10] For children with no parents, no food, and no money, school is an impossible dream.

It destroys families, communities, even generations. Most of us have the luxury of a place we call home. We enjoy the comfort of family members who care about us or for us. We have family members or friends who will be there for us in good times and in bad. Our children play with our neighbor's children. We live in a society where family and community are *assumptions*, not exceptions. What if all of that were gone?

Twelve million African children have already lost one or both parents to AIDS, and unless we take serious action now, there will be more than eighteen million AIDS orphans by the end of the decade.[11] The disease has wiped out anything resembling a nuclear family.

When I was in Africa, I could hardly believe what these communities had been reduced to. Many small children ran free in the streets, but there were few adults. Small, one-room huts that were meant for a family of four were instead packed, sardine-like, with twenty-five orphaned children! Sometimes, I would spot a "gogo," a grandma who was working with the kids. But there were no men and few teenagers. Graves littered the hillsides.

Children have lost friends and families. They have no one to feed them or to look after them. Before HIV slapped them in the face, these people were already living in poverty. Now many people groups, villages, and tribes are on the brink of extinction.

THE GREATEST CRISIS

Experts tell us World War II killed 62 million people.[12] Even with all of the advances in medicine, AIDS continues on a path to eclipse that number, having already killed 25 million people since the first case in 1981. The UN estimates that 39.5 million people are now living with HIV. Of that total, 4.3 million were new infections in 2006. There were 2.9 million AIDS deaths in 2006, the highest number reported in any year.[13]

How do you describe a crisis like this? Catastrophic? Disastrous? Devastating?

Words just can't paint an accurate picture of what this disease is doing to our world. Dr. Peter Piot, the executive director of UNAIDS, said, "Countries are not moving at the same speed as their epidemics." Without rapid improvements, the pandemic will only worsen, the officials said.[14] This is the greatest crisis humanity has ever faced.

IT GETS WORSE

While it is true that HIV is spread though unprotected sex and intravenous drug use, these are not the only ways the disease is proliferated. Sadly, the other primary means of spreading the disease impacts the innocent.

One of the first children I met in Africa was a little girl named Nobile. Nobile is a beautiful, sweet nine-year-old from Swaziland. We saw her first from a distance, admiring her smile and charisma.

The caretaker of the children's center noticed how we were lauding over Nobile and told us her story. A year earlier, Nobile was visiting a few of the programs at Hawane, a local ministry that cares for children. One of the workers there learned that Nobile was left home alone all day and decided to start bringing her in the afternoons so she could spend time with children her age and receive educational training.

As days passed, workers began to notice that Nobile frequently wet herself. She was ashamed and would often run away crying. Initially workers were shocked to think that this little girl had never been potty-trained. But when they took her to a doctor, what they learned turned their shock into horror, anger, and despair.

Nobile didn't lack the training to control her bladder. She had been so violently raped that she was *unable* to control her bladder. Both of Nobile's parents had died from AIDS. With no one to protect her, she had become a prime target for a nearby relative—her uncle.

Thanks to the programs of Hawane, Nobile is now safe. She lives in a home where she is well taken care of by people who love her. But she is just one little girl. One of many who are suffering because of this horrible disease.

THE AIDS STIGMA

Stories like Nobile's are horribly difficult to hear. Most of us really can't comprehend the brutality and the pain of such a circumstance. But no matter how difficult these sorts of stories are, it's still much easier to have compassion for innocent victims like Nobile than for the multitude of people who are sick because of their own choices. Because of (wait for it) … sin.

For some of you, this may be the heart of the issue. How are we, as Christians, supposed to respond to this disease? Before we go there, let's clear up a few lies that get in the way of a proper response.

The following are blatant lies about HIV:

You can contract HIV by sitting on a toilet seat.

You can get HIV from a water fountain or from someone else's saliva. (You'd have to drink a five-gallon bucket's worth of spit to stand a chance. Any takers?)

Only homosexuals or drug users get AIDS.

You can tell by looking at people if they're infected by HIV.

Debunking lies is easy. The truth, on the other hand, is not. Yes, the majority of people with HIV got it through sexual contact or because of drug use. But does that make them less worthy of compassion?

It seems as if we have taken a hands-off approach to this disease because people classify it, at best, as a dirty disease and, at worst, as a curse from God. But how might Jesus have responded to AIDS?

Obviously, AIDS is a new disease, not something Jesus would have encountered when he walked this earth. He did, however, encounter leprosy, which was considered a dirty disease at the time. Sure, there are some differences, but let's not get tripped up by that. Take a moment to look at leprosy. It doesn't require a time machine to see what it's like—leprosy is still with us today. My friend Kari visited two leper colonies, and here's what she had to say.

> One of the colonies was built on a sewage pond, where the smell seeps out of the ground and rises over the whole colony. Swarms of kids and flies followed us through the streets. The kids wore ragged, dirty clothes, no shoes, and sometimes no pants. They probably do not remember the last time they were bathed. They run wild through the colony, as most of their parents are sick and many are confined to straw mats and cannot walk.
>
> It's not a pretty picture. Leprosy is a hideous, visceral disease that rots the skin right off of the body. Many people would be sickened or even horrified in the presence of a leper. Not Jesus. "A leper came to him [Jesus], begging on his knees, 'If you want to, you can cleanse me.' Deeply moved, Jesus put out his hand, touched him, and said, 'I want to. Be clean.' Then and there the leprosy was gone, his skin smooth and healthy" (Mark 1:40–42).

Jesus didn't walk on the other side of the road. He didn't scrunch up his face in disgust or withhold his hand. He reached out with love and compassion. I'm humbled and proud to say Kari and her team did the same. Here's more of her account:

> The lepers bowed to us in humility, clasping their nubbed fingers together in a sign of respect. As we were faced with the choice of whether or not to shake the nubby hands, no one on the team held back. I can't describe how it feels to clasp the disfigured hand of a leper. It feels like *love* in a way I have never felt before. We all know that our Father would hold these people in his arms. We wanted to be him to these people who needed to know his love.

In most societies you'll find groups of people whom others deem untouchable. They go by many names—the unclean, the poor, the cursed, the trash of society. Lepers surely fall into this category. And, whether out of ignorance or embarrassment, many people today would quietly shuffle those suffering from AIDS into that "untouchable" category as well.

From a spiritual perspective, this category isn't the horrible place we might think it to be. Untouchables hold a very special place in the heart of God. He is their rescuer, their defender, and he is the one who takes up their cause.

And that's where we come in. We are God's hands. What God cares about, we ought to care about. No matter how poor, no matter how down and out, no matter how untouchable people are, as

Christ-followers we are to reach out to them (just like Kari and her team) with compassion. We are to do the work Jesus commands us to do—feed the hungry, heal the sick, provide shelter for the homeless.

Jesus walked this earth to bring the kingdom of God down from heaven. He came to bring salvation and to right wrongs. There is a beautiful example of this "righting of wrongs" in the gospel of Mark. In chapter 9, Jesus was presented with a boy who was possessed by some kind of evil spirit. Though many had tried, no one had been able to help the boy, and people had begun to fear him. His father came to Jesus pleading for help: "A man out of the crowd answered, 'Teacher, I brought my mute son, made speechless by a demon, to you. Whenever it seizes him, it throws him to the ground. He foams at the mouth, grinds his teeth, and goes stiff as a board. I told your disciples, hoping they could deliver him, but they couldn't'" (Mark 9:17–18).

I am amazed at these kinds of passages, because of what Jesus does. He was arguably one of the busiest people of his time. He had things to do, important kingdom business to accomplish in a short thirty-three years. And yet every time he encountered a need, he stopped what he was doing and met the need.

That's because this *was* kingdom business. Nothing was more important to Jesus than meeting real needs in the lives of real people. I imagine that this young boy who was foaming at the mouth and throwing fits scared more than a few people to the opposite side of the road, each of them silently choosing their excuse from a virtual spreadsheet of seemingly reasonable options, such as,

"What if he's contagious?" or "I wouldn't know what to do," or "It's not my problem," or "He must be a sinner." Jesus didn't cross to the other side of the road. He saw the need and, regardless of the story that brought that young boy into his difficult circumstance, responded to him with love. Jesus was the living example of the good Samaritan. We are called to imitate his life. Paul said it this way:

> In light of all this, here's what I want you to do. While I'm locked up here, a prisoner for the Master, I want you to get out there and walk—better yet, run!—on the road God called you to travel. I don't want any of you sitting around on your hands. I don't want anyone strolling off, down some path that goes nowhere. And mark that you do this with humility and discipline—not in fits and starts, but steadily, pouring yourselves out for each other in acts of love, alert at noticing differences and quick at mending fences. (Eph. 4:1–3)

Picture Jesus walking down the streets of Jerusalem. What moved his heart? Where was his compassion revealed? What received most of his attention? The needs of the poor, the down and out, the handicapped, the orphan, the prostitute, and the widow. Over and over again, this is where Jesus poured out his life. He didn't do this out of duty or requirement. He didn't stop to ask what led the people to their place of pain or need. He reached out because his heart was overflowing with compassion. He made other men and women's sorrows his sorrows and other people's suffering his suffering,

We're to follow in his footsteps.

Does it matter how someone contracted HIV? Yes, I suppose it does. But not in the way you might be thinking. We are not called to judge. To educate? To inform? To teach? Yes. All of these things are good. But more than anything else, we are called to reach out in compassion. We are called to touch the untouchables. And it is that very touch—a touch not unlike that offered by Jesus—that gives hope.

THE OVERWHELMING TRUTH

Africa isn't the only place being devastated by this disease. Russia is facing the largest HIV epidemic in Europe, and accounts for around two-thirds of the cases in the eastern Europe and central Asia regions. An estimated 940,000 people in Russia were living with HIV at the end of 2005.

Epidemiologists warn that up to eight million Russians, or over 10 percent of the adult population, could be infected by 2010. The epidemic is growing fastest among young people ages fifteen to thirty, the same group that should be leading Russia into the twenty-first century.[15]

In Asia, an estimated 8.6 million people are living with HIV, an increase of nearly one million, and 630,000 people died from AIDS-related illnesses in that vast region this year. India, where the epidemic appears to be stable or diminishing in some parts while growing modestly in others, has 5.7 million infected people, most of whom contracted the disease through heterosexual sex. In China, where the epidemic was first seen in rural areas, a large number of migrants (an estimated 120 to 150 million) could spread the virus even further.[16] There are nearly one million people in the United States who are infected by HIV, and a quarter of them don't even know it. AIDS is affecting almost every country in the world—and it could get worse.

Okay. Take a breath. Allow yourself to be overwhelmed. That's a normal response. Our minds can't comprehend a problem this big. Sure, we can see that it's horrible. We can feel the waves of sadness and despair pouring out from the hearts of the afflicted. But it's all too much.

Of course it is. It's too much for me. Too much for you. Too much for any one individual to tackle. But that's not what I'm asking. That's not what anyone is asking. Think about Nobile's story. Think about Happiness's story. These are real people with real stories. And we are too. This is how we can make a difference. Each of us, through one act of kindness, can play out our own story— one that changes the life of one person in Africa. I love the slogan my friends at The Chronicle Project came up with: "Everyone Makes a Difference: If everyone does one thing for one issue, the world would be an entirely different place."

That's what this book is about. A different world. One defined not by despair and disease, but defined by the product of compassion: hope.

And a lawyer stood up and put Him to the test, saying, "Teacher, what shall I do to inherit eternal life?"

And He said to him, "What is written in the Law? How does it read to you?"

And he answered, "You shall love the Lord your God with all your heart, and with all your soul, and with all your strength, and with all your mind; and your neighbor as yourself."

And He said to him, "You have answered correctly; do this and you will live."

—Luke 10:25–28 NASB

AN INADEQUATE RESPONSE

ADANNA'S NAME IS a beautiful African word meaning "father's daughter." But Adanna won't live until the next harvest season unless something drastic happens. In her home country of Zimbabwe, there are no jobs, there is no money, and the only thing certain is the death that surrounds her.

The expected life span for people in her country is only thirty-three.[1] She has watched her mother, her father, and her sister waste away to AIDS. Adanna is now in charge of her family. She is the head of the household.

She is ten years old.

Adanna's parents left no way for her to care for herself and the rest of the family. She has exhausted every favor from her neighbors, every form of assistance from surviving relatives, and sold her last possession for food. But she and her brother and sister woke up starving again this morning.

There is only one way for them to survive. Adanna has heard about a group of local men who will trade food for sex. Dare she even consider such a thing? For all of her young life she has dreamed of someday having a family of her own. She has protected her purity because she wants the man she marries to be the only lover she ever knows. Her mother taught her this.

Adanna's dreams and her purity mean everything to her, but if she doesn't eat soon, neither will matter. She will be dead.

Children grow up fast in Africa. She makes a decision. A terrible, necessary decision. She goes to these men. Perhaps they'll have compassion for her. Perhaps they'll give her food without asking anything in return. They look at her, they grab her, they fondle her, and they laugh. They refuse to give her food. "Why should we give you anything, you ugly little mongrel?" they shout.

They tell her to go into the back room of the store and wait. She steps into a room that smells of urine and mold. She is shaking. A sickly man is sleeping in the corner.

Suddenly, three men come in drinking and shouting. They approach her not as a human being but as a mere animal. She screams. She cries. Nobody is listening. Nobody cares.

And they steal her dreams.

She leaves with food. Enough to keep her alive. But what kind of life? She has just contracted HIV. She will die of AIDS within three years.

SOFTENING A HARDENED HEART

I suspect as you read about Adanna, her story broke your heart. Perhaps it horrified you or made you angry. But what will happen to those emotions as the day wears on? As the week progresses? Will they fade away? And what will flow into the space vacated by those emotions? Indifference? Helplessness?

The news media fires global statistics at us like bullets from a machine gun. They approach quickly, growing larger than life and demanding our attention. But they just as quickly pass by, or even through us, leaving little more than a rapidly decaying whiff of the incomprehensible truth that ignited them in the first place.

We *need* to see the statistics. We need to examine the scope of the problems we're facing before we can begin to respond to them. But statistics can also immobilize us, nail our feet to the floor. The feeling of being overwhelmed is one of the greatest obstacles you and I face when we begin to think about what we should do— what we *can* do—to make a difference.

The second-greatest obstacle is our own breakneck existence. How many plates are you spinning today? We live in a culture that is defined by plate-spinning. I don't know about you, but the prospect of adding yet another plate scares me sometimes. The ones I've already got spinning—the Family Plate, the Friends Plate, the Job Plate—some of them are teetering already. Can I really add the Africa Plate today?

And so it happens. Whether because we feel overwhelmed or busy, we slowly or swiftly slip into the only place where Africa's problems don't cry out to us. We slip into apathy. We don't always mean to. "Of course I care about Africa. Of course I care about little Adanna. But … but … I'm sorry, I've just got to get back to my other plates."

Eleanor Roosevelt once said, "So much attention is paid to the aggressive sins, such as violence and cruelty and greed with all their tragic effects, that too little attention is paid to the passive sins, such as apathy and laziness, which in the long run can have a more devastating effect."

Listen, I'm not trying to dump a guilt trip on us here. We've all slipped into apathy about life or the needs of others at one time or another. It's an easy thing to do. But there is a more important issue here. Namely, the kingdom of God. The questions we must ask are, "How does God view our apathy?" and, "What is the response God desires from us as we consider the needs of the world?" The answer is found in a familiar parable. I've referenced it once already. And you probably could recite it from memory yourself. But look at it again.

> Just then a religion scholar stood up with a question to test
> Jesus. "Teacher, what do I need to do to get eternal life?"

He answered, "What's written in God's Law? How do you interpret it?"

He said, "That you love the Lord your God with all your passion and prayer and muscle and intelligence— and that you love your neighbor as well as you do yourself."

"Good answer!" said Jesus. "Do it and you'll live."

Looking for a loophole, he asked, "And just how would you define 'neighbor'?"

Jesus answered by telling a story. "There was once a man traveling from Jerusalem to Jericho. On the way he was attacked by robbers. They took his clothes, beat him up, and went off leaving him half-dead. Luckily, a priest was on his way down the same road, but when he saw him he angled across to the other side. Then a Levite religious man showed up; he also avoided the injured man.

"A Samaritan traveling the road came on him. When he saw the man's condition, his heart went out to him. He gave him first aid, disinfecting and bandaging his wounds. Then he lifted him onto his donkey, led him to an inn, and made him comfortable. In the morning he took out two silver coins and gave them to the innkeeper, saying, 'Take good care of him. If it costs any more, put it on my bill—I'll pay you on my way back.'

"What do you think? Which of the three became a neighbor to the man attacked by robbers?"

"The one who treated him kindly," the religion scholar responded.

Jesus said, "Go and do the same." (Luke 10:25–37)

I find it interesting that Jesus juxtaposed two supposed religious people, a priest and a Levite, against a worldly "dog" of a man (the Samaritan) in this narrative. But I don't think he meant for us to get too caught up in the comparison between those who had a whole bunch of gold stars on their religious report cards and a man who was reviled by the Jews. Surely the choice of these particular characters was intentional, perhaps a means not only to keep his listeners' attention but also to chip away (as Jesus often did) at the "old way" of thinking, where religiosity ruled. But I wonder if some listeners would have been distracted by Jesus' choice of characters and missed his greater point: What matters most is having a heart that goes out to those in need and then *acting* on that need.

The religious leaders who were listening to Jesus probably came up with their own excuses for why the priest and Levite did nothing. "Maybe they were late for meetings; maybe they thought someone else would be a better source of help. But surely they at least felt sorry for the man, right?" Perhaps. But it was only the Samaritan whose heart went out to the man and who took action on that heart tug. Because of the Samaritan's hands-dirty work, the man by the side of the road received medical help and was cared for in ways he could not have accomplished on his own. He was given hope.

This isn't just a story about being nice to your neighbor or even merely a story about determining *who* is your neighbor. It's a story about doing the work of God's kingdom—the work that leads to hope. The work that leads to life.

LIES AND SHADOWS

An eighteenth-century English philosopher named Edmund Burke once said, "The only thing necessary for the triumph of evil is for good men [and women] to do nothing." Doesn't this look just a little bit like the message of Jesus' parable? If we apply it to the HIV/AIDS crisis, it doesn't take much of a leap to see how evil triumphs when good men and women sit on the sidelines while Africa burns and crumbles.

So why don't we do more to help others? Sadly, many of us live in a world of shadows. In the realm of shadows, we seek only those things that help us to remain in the fog of comfort and safety. This isn't to say that comfort and safety are bad things, but when we fall into the trance of believing they are the *only* things, we become isolated from greater truths. Two things keep us in the shadows: discomfort with interruption and fear.

As a culture, we don't do well with interruption. Interruption brings change, and change is uncomfortable. Imagine you have a close friend whose marriage is on the brink of divorce. (Sadly, this may not take much imagination.) Do you leap at the chance to be there for your friend and lend a helping hand that could possibly save the marriage? Or is your first response to shrink back, to hide in the shadows, consider your own relational issues, and then do little more than pray for your friend's marriage?

And then there is fear. Fear is almost as pervasive in our culture as Starbucks or Wal-Mart. Only in a culture where fear rules would an action-sports company find huge success marketing its brand with only two words: No Fear. We are a culture predicated on fear. But what are we afraid of? Loss. Loss of our jobs, financial loss, the loss of friends, our reputations, and even ourselves.

Fear brings all of the "what ifs" to the surface: What if I become too involved in someone else's life and I lose something from my own life? What if it costs money? What if the stories break my heart? What if it costs me my life? What if? What if? What if? Line up enough of these "what ifs" and they start to tower over us, placing us … you guessed it … back in the shadows.

Well, what if you didn't wake up tomorrow? What if a tornado wiped out your house? What if you were in a terrible accident next week? The "what if" life is a paralyzed life, an imprisoned life.

Fear keeps us from acting on the compassion in our hearts. It also keeps us from receiving what we desperately need in our own lives. However, when we give greatly to others, we receive tremendous blessings back into our lives. Jesus said, "Give away your life; you'll find life given back, but not merely given back—given back with bonus and blessing. Giving, not getting, is the way. Generosity begets generosity" (Luke 6:38).

Sir Winston Churchill said it this way: "We make a living by what we get, but we make a life by what we give." If we open our lives to the needs of other people and our world, we receive in ways that boggle the mind. I'm not saying your generosity toward others will earn you first prize in the lottery or a date with that man or woman of your dreams. I'm talking about receiving the intangibles that really matter—peace, grace, love, hope, and purpose.

God makes this "deal" with us in the Bible: "If you take care of the things that are on my heart, I'll take care of the things on yours." Not a bad arrangement if you're paying attention to the things that matter to God. The Bible is filled with verses that talk about this very thing. For example, Psalm 37:4 (NASB) says, "Delight yourself in the LORD; and He will give you the desires of your heart."

This is one of the main principles I talk about in my book *Fields of the Fatherless.* As God gave the Israelites instructions on how to live, he not only told them what they were supposed to do, but what he would do in return: "When you reap your harvest in your field and have forgotten a sheaf in the field, you shall not go back to get it; it shall be for the alien, for the orphan, and for the widow, in order that the LORD your God may bless you in all the work of your hands" (Deut. 24:19 NASB).

Simply put, if you take care of the needs of the alien, the orphan, and the widow, God will bless what you do. Nobody takes care of the needs of the poor only to get a blessing from God. That's not the point. The point is that God won't hang you out to dry if you have a compassionate heart. Quite the opposite.

Every time I go into a community to offer help, I take with me little more than a sincere desire to do whatever is needed. I go with the expectation that I will leave a little of my money, my time—a little of myself—with people who need it more than I do. I don't do this to get anything in return—I do it because it delights God. But here's the crazy truth: Every time I leave that kind of environment, I walk away with far more than I gave. I walk away with the smiles I saw in people's eyes, with the echoing laughter from the mouths of children. I walk away changed. The apostle Paul understood this principle and lived it out wholeheartedly: "In everything I showed you that by working hard in this manner you must help the weak and remember the words of the Lord Jesus, that He Himself said, 'It is more blessed to give than to receive'" (Acts 20:35 NASB).

In some situations, you and I may be the only people who have the power to make a difference. The child sponsorship program we have at Children's HopeChest brings this issue to light. Some people considering this program ask this difficult, yet honest question: "How can I sponsor a child infected with HIV who I know is going to die?" I suppose only the person asking the question can really answer it. But here's what I know: If you sponsor a child who is only on this earth for a short time more, you may be the *only* person in the world they know who loves them, cares about them, and will miss them when they're gone. Isn't that reason enough?

THE INADEQUATE RESPONSE OF THE CHURCH

Africa is a continent bursting into flames, and the church's response has been far too inadequate for far too long. As Bono said, "We've got watering cans, when what we really need are the fire brigades."[2] As Christ-followers, we have a theological understanding of both evil and redemption. This understanding ought to compel us to show the world how to respond to suffering and indifference.

Jesus knew the dangers of getting caught up in religiosity. (Jump back a few pages and read that Samaritan story again, and you'll see what I mean.) And he wasn't afraid to speak his mind on such matters because Jesus had only one thing on his heart: what mattered most to his Father. Jesus cared about his followers *being* the kingdom of God to their fellow brothers and sisters in need. He cared about believers obeying the Word of God and loving their neighbors as much as they loved themselves.

Ah yes, Jesus' followers. The church. You. Me. Us. It pains me to say that we, as a church, have thus far failed to live up to Jesus' hope for our "being" the kingdom of God when it comes to the crisis in Africa. Don't misunderstand me. There are lots of good people doing great things to make a difference in Africa. But the Samaritans are the people on the frontlines rallying the world's help. Rock stars, high-profile actors, and secular humanitarians have stepped up to the plate with actions to match their words, while the church has been sitting quietly (if uncomfortably) on the sidelines. Thank God for Samaritans.

Shouldn't we, as Christ-followers, be the first-response team for any humanitarian crisis? We, of all people, ought to know better. We preach God's love for the *whole world*. It's not like we black out those sections in our Bibles that speak of Jesus' immense care and concern for the orphan and the widow. We know it. We talk about it. But how well do we live it? Consider what James 2:14–17 says:

> Dear friends, do you think you'll get anywhere in this if you learn all the right words but never do anything? Does merely talking about faith indicate that a person really has it? For instance, you come upon an old friend dressed in rags and half-starved and say, "Good morning, friend! Be clothed in Christ! Be filled with the Holy Spirit!" and walk off without providing so much as a coat or a cup of soup—where does that get you? Isn't it obvious that God-talk without God-acts is outrageous nonsense?

As Christ-followers, we need to step to the front of the line. We need to lead the charge. There are many specific, tangible ways we can do this. Keep reading—you'll land in a pool of them in later chapters. But before getting too wet, it's important to grasp the reason for that leap. This isn't just about "doing our little part" to make a difference. It's about moving forward, putting into motion the mission God has given us. We are Jesus, his hands extended. We are his voice of love. We are his feet. Where would Jesus be today? What poorest-of-the-poor people would he walk among, offering his healing touch and life-giving hope? That's where I want to be.

This is not a new mission. It's not a new journey. In fact, the church used to be well known for the manner in which they reached out to those in need. Christ-followers who lived in the second and third centuries were leaders in caring for the poor. Many even created "how-to" manuals for recent converts, offering them practical instruction on how to reach out to those in need. One of these documents, the *Didache* (perhaps written around 100 CE), instructed Christians to "give to everyone who asks thee, and do not refuse." Similarly, *The Shepherd of Hermas* (early 100s) instructed Christians to "give simply to all without asking doubtfully to whom thou givest but give to all." In the early 200s, Tertullian reported that Christians had a voluntary common fund into which they monthly deposited what they could. The common fund was used to support widows, the disabled, orphans, the sick, the elderly, shipwrecked sailors, prisoners, teachers, burials for the poor, and even for the release of slaves.[3]

As early as the second century, Christians were practicing a unique and sacrificial form of charity. They would fast and give the unconsumed food and resources to the poor and hungry. This is mentioned in *The Shepherd of Hermas*:

> Having fulfilled what is written, in the day on which you fast you will taste nothing but bread and water; and having reckoned up the price of the dishes of that day which you intended to have eaten, you will give it to a widow, or an orphan, or to some person in want, and thus you will exhibit humility of mind, so that he who has received benefit from your humility may fill his own soul, and pray for you to the Lord.[4]

It seems our "church" has been formed and reformed and shaped and reshaped and cluttered to the point that it is practically unrecognizable. I wonder what the first-century Christians would say if they could see the church today? I have often wondered what today's church might look like stripped of all the excess. I don't mean to disparage church movements or the many good things that the church is doing, but I wonder how much digging it would take to find the church in its purest form—people whose love and compassion for God overflows into the lives of the most needy.

In his book *Under the Influence*, Alvin Schmidt presented a history of the early church. Can you guess what he talks about over and over? You got it. A love for the poor and the orphan, a passion for the sanctity of life, fighting for the rights of women so they wouldn't be treated as second-class citizens; it's all in there.

And there's more. Justin Martyr, an early defender of Christianity, described how collections were taken in church services to help the orphans. Another church father, Tertullian, reported that the church in Carthage, Africa, had a common treasury to aid the orphaned children. In the sixth, seventh, and eighth centuries, Italian bishops and clergy "zealously defended widows and orphans."[5]

Maybe the manner in which we meet is different. Maybe we've traded our lutes for electric guitars, our scrolls for PowerPoint presentations. But we are still the church! We are still God's people. Loving the outcast and the downtrodden and the hopeless is in the very DNA of the kingdom.

Listen, dear friends. Isn't it clear by now that God oper-
ates quite differently? He chose the world's down-and-out
as the kingdom's first citizens, with full rights and privi-
leges. This kingdom is promised to anyone who loves
God. And here you are abusing these same citizens! Isn't it
the high and mighty who exploit you, who use the courts
to rob you blind? Aren't they the ones who scorn the new
name—"Christian"—used in your baptisms? (James
2:5–7)

What we're after is one simple word: *transformation*—of our
personal lives and the lives of the world's most needy. That's the
essence of the kingdom, and nothing else can satisfy our dry souls.

First things first. Your business is life, not death. Follow me. Pursue life.

—Matthew 8:22

THE
SANCTITY
OF LIFE

O NE OF THE most moving experiences I've had was attending the first ever HIV/AIDS conference held at Saddleback Church. That's Rick Warren's church—you may know him as the author of *The Purpose Driven Life*. The conference was the vision of Rick's wife, Kay.

I was standing in the back of the auditorium when Rick told a story that struck me to the core. He was talking about those direct-mail cards we sometimes get. Shuffled in among the offers for new siding or half-price dinners or time-share properties is a card featuring a picture of a young missing child and the caption, "Have You Seen Me?" I'm sure you know what I'm referring to. And I'm also sure you've done what I've done with these cards: toss them in the trash.

That's what Rick did. He let his flutter to the bottom of the garbage can. As he glanced down, he saw the face of a beautiful little girl looking up at him. In that moment, God spoke to him: "What if that was *your* little girl?"

This caught Rick's attention. Mine, too. You see, I have six kids from ages nineteen all the way down to one. What if the picture on that card was one of my babies? I couldn't even imagine such a thing. How would I feel? What would I do? What would *you* do if it was one of your children or grandchildren, or a niece or nephew, or just a girl or boy you called a friend?

I think we would all do the same thing. We'd do anything within our power to find our child. I asked the question earlier, "How does God feel about these children who are suffering?" The same way you and I would feel if one of our children were lost and in pain. Every child behind the tragic statistics we've included in this book belongs to God. They are his sons and daughters.

Psalm 139:13–16 presents this truth beautifully:

> Oh yes, you shaped me first inside, then out;
>> you formed me in my mother's womb.
> I thank you, High God—you're breathtaking!
> Body and soul, I am marvelously made!
>> I worship in adoration—what a creation!

You know me inside and out, you know every bone in
my body;
You know exactly how I was made, bit by bit,
how I was sculpted from nothing into something.
Like an open book, you watched me grow from concep-
tion to birth.

WHY WE HAVE TO CARE

Since God cares about people to this depth, we have a moral, biblical obligation to do the same. When we enter the kingdom of
God, we join a family. Our whole world changes. The things we
used to care about don't matter so much. Instead, we are privileged
to care about the things God cares about. What matters to him
matters to us.

There's nothing more important on God's agenda than caring
for the sick and the hurting, the poor and the orphan. There's
nothing more rewarding than giving our lives to those who need
the most help.

Remember what I said in chapter 1? God closely identifies
himself with the poor. According to Matthew 25, he *is* the poor.
I've always found this passage fascinating. It doesn't say, "When
you clothe the naked, feed the poor, and visit the sick it means a
lot to God, he's happy, and it's 'sort of like' doing it to him." It says
when we do those kinds of things, we do them *to him*. He *is* them.
I think it's pretty clear that this means following Christ is all about
helping the outcast.

How serious is God about this? Well, the hard-to-swallow part of Matthew 25 shows us. I don't like to think about this passage much because it's not very pretty. But it is real. And it is God's truth.

> Then he will turn to the "goats," the ones on his left, and say, "Get out, worthless goats! You're good for nothing but the fires of hell. And why? Because—
> I was hungry and you gave me no meal,
> I was thirsty and you gave me no drink,
> I was homeless and you gave me no bed,
> I was shivering and you gave me no clothes,
> Sick and in prison, and you never visited."
> Then those "goats" are going to say, "Master, what are you talking about? When did we ever see you hungry or thirsty or homeless or shivering or sick or in prison and didn't help?"
> He will answer them, "I'm telling the solemn truth: Whenever you failed to do one of these things to someone who was being overlooked or ignored, that was me—you failed to do it to me." (Matt. 25:41–45)

Those who ignore the needs of the hungry, the prisoner, and the orphan will have to account for their behavior one day. Apparently, God's not going to think very well of them. In just these few paragraphs where Jesus talked about heaven, he told us everything we need to know about how to live our life today. He told us what's high on God's priority list and what that means for how we should live.

What if there is a huge secret about what it means to "work out our salvation" in this verse? What if a life of faith is all about what Jesus was saying here? Can you imagine! I don't think this is so far-fetched. Perhaps it's why Jesus put so much emphasis on these verses. When asked by his disciples what will happen at the end of this age, Jesus didn't speak of the thunderous applause of angels or of being ushered into beautiful huge mansions. Instead, he set the scene of a one-on-one interview with Jesus himself asking only one important question: "How well did you take care of the people I love?"

If this is true, then those heavenly transcripts that list what we did for the poor, the needy, and the suffering will show evidence of whether or not our Bible study, our discipleship groups, our quiet times, and our pew-sitting actually moved the short distance from our head down into our heart. Jesus is serious about this. I love this quote by Richard Rohr from his book *From Wild Man to Wise Man*:

> I would say that if you only think about Jesus, "believe" Jesus and believe things about Jesus, not much new is going to happen. It is the risk of "acting" like Jesus acted that reconfigures your soul. We are converted by new circumstances much more than by new ideas. Or as I like to say, *we do not think ourselves into new ways of living, we live ourselves into new ways of thinking.*[1]

A HOPE AND A FUTURE

One of my favorite passages of Scripture is Jeremiah 29:11–14. I can't tell you how many times I quoted it while in Bible college. Jeremiah's words gave me hope. They reminded me I had a destiny.

> I know what I'm doing. I have it all planned out—plans to take care of you, not abandon you, plans to give you the future you hope for. When you call on me, when you come and pray to me, I'll listen. When you come looking for me, you'll find me. Yes, when you get serious about finding me and want it more than anything else, I'll make sure you won't be disappointed.

When I was nineteen, I had a rap sheet a mile long and problems more numerous than the grains of sand in the Sahara. After partying all night and drinking several bottles of over-the-counter cough medicine, my friends and I decided to drive around town. We were enjoying the time-tested, drug-and-alcohol-influenced "fun" of making obscene gestures at people we encountered along the side of the road. As we slowed to yell our best obscenities at one woman, she looked directly at me and said, "Do you know God loves you and has a wonderful plan for your life?" I opened my mouth to spit the crudest word I could think of, and … nothing. It wouldn't come out. I looked at my friends. They, too, were rendered speechless by the power of this woman's words. We were so freaked out we cut the party short and hurried home with our tails between our legs.

I made it to Bible school in part because I couldn't get the woman's words out of my head. When I discovered this passage in Jeremiah, I understood why those words were so powerful: They're God's own words.

As I've come to recognize the diversity of living conditions and circumstances in our world, I've had to ask myself some tough questions: *Does this Jeremiah passage apply to everyone or just to those of us who live in wealthy countries? Does it pack the same kind of meaning to people in developing countries; do they get to look forward to a hope and a future? Does it apply to the infant who was just infected with HIV through her mother's breast milk? Does Adanna get to claim this promise of a God-ordained destiny?*

God says, "I will not abandon you." Put yourself into the figurative shoes (she has no real ones) of a five-year-old girl somewhere in the middle of Africa. Your father has died of AIDS and, after you've watched your mother cough up blood and shrivel to nothing for the last month and a half, she, too, is gone. How do you make sense of this passage? How could you not feel abandoned?

What do you set your hopes in? You set your hopes in people. People who might show up and offer a refuge, a safe place, a home. People who are the living embodiment of Christ himself. People like you and me. People who can show, with the actions of their heart, that God has not abandoned you at all.

God created every human being in his image, including people like this five-year-old girl whom the rest of the world has thrown away because of cruelty or neglect or indifference. God has plans for each of them to have hope and a future too. Here's what I'm getting at—God does not abandon us. But sometimes, it takes the touch of God-with-skin-on to remind us of that. Perhaps you've had seasons when the silence of God has echoed loudly in your heart. How did you find your way back? I expect the encouragement and prayers of others helped. And that's who we are to be to the poor and hurting in Africa—*others*. God's others. God has given us the tools and the resources to give hope to the hopeless. But unless we take those tools out of the closet, millions of innocent men, women, and children will continue to die without knowing that hope.

This is about life. And it is about something else, too: justice.

God's Spirit is on me; he's chosen
me to preach the Message of
good news to the poor,

Sent me to announce pardon to prisoners
and recovery of sight to the blind,

To set the burdened and battered free, to
announce, "This is God's year to act!"

—Luke 4:18–19

A CALL TO
JUSTICE

SPEAKING AT THE U.S. national prayer breakfast, Bono
said something amazing about the AIDS issue and Africa.

> This is not about charity in the end, is it? It's about jus-
> tice. The good news yet to come. I just want to repeat

that: This is not about charity, it's about justice. And that's too bad. Because we're good at charity. Americans, Irish people, are good at charity. We like to give, and we give a lot, even those who can't afford it.

But justice is a higher standard. Africa makes a fool of our idea of justice; it makes a farce of our idea of equality. It mocks our pieties; it doubts our concern, and it questions our commitment. Six and a half thousand Africans are still dying every day of preventable, treatable disease, for lack of drugs we can buy at any drug store. This is not about charity: This is about Justice and Equality.[1]

I began to truly understand this idea of justice when I started visiting orphans in Russia. Here were little boys and girls who had dreams and hopes for a good life, kids just like my kids. They looked like my kids, laughed like my kids, and played like my kids.

But, through no fault of their own, they were abandoned and relegated to a scary, cold, and lonely existence in an orphanage. They would be kicked out of that miserable place at fifteen or sixteen, but this was no great escape into a world of possibilities. Sixty percent of the girls would become prostitutes. Seventy percent of the boys would end up on the street or in jail.

Do you hear what I hear? It's a voice crying out from inside, and it's saying, "That's not right! It isn't fair!" It is a voice crying for justice.

In India, the caste system rules. Your birth, and *only* your birth, determines which caste you fall under. If you're of a low caste, you will spend the rest of your life being subservient to those who are a higher caste. The best jobs are reserved for the high caste, as are the best governmental positions and all places of honor.

There is a group of people in India, a group 250 million strong, called the Dalit. For three millennia, the Dalit have been labeled as so worthless they aren't even allowed to be part of the caste system. If the shadow of a Dalit girl so much as falls on a member of a higher caste, she will be mercilessly beaten as punishment for polluting the higher caste. The Dalit are little more than slaves to the rest of the population. By the time Dalit children are five or six years old, they know they're the trash of their society. They know they're worthless, stupid, good for nothing. And they also know they're easy targets for those who wish to take advantage of their invisible status. Over a million children are missing in India because they have been maimed, tortured, sold into the sex-trade industry, raped, or killed.[2]

Not long ago, a Dalit lady who had rightful ownership to a piece of land was confronted by a member of a higher caste who wanted to take that land away from her. Because of his position, he believed he had the right to take it.

After the woman filed the proper paperwork in court to prove her rightful ownership of the property, the man became enraged. He gathered a group together and confronted her outside her home. She and her children were dragged out of the house as her husband watched. There the men sodomized and

raped the children, sodomized and raped the woman, then bru-
tally murdered them with swords and knives.

As of this writing, no charges have been brought against these
men—simply because of their social status. This, my friends, is
injustice. Do you hear that voice now? It's practically screaming,
"This is not right! Something must be done!"

Yes, indeed. Something must be done. We are biblically obli-
gated to defend those who live as modern-day slaves, who have
been abandoned, who have no one to defend them and no one to
turn to.

WHAT IS JUSTICE?

Justice is giving to those who have nothing. Biblical justice is
about making sure the weak are protected from abuse and showing the love of God in a practical, tangible way. It is about those
who _have_ giving to those who _have not._

Justice is action. It means making wrongs right, bringing
blessing instead of curse, and giving our lives to serve others in
need. Without action, what we do lacks power. Look again at
James 2:14–17:

> Dear friends, do you think you'll get anywhere in this if
> you learn all the right words but never do anything? Does
> merely talking about faith indicate that a person really has
> it? For instance, you come upon an old friend dressed in
> rags and half-starved and say, "Good morning, friend! Be

clothed in Christ! Be filled with the Holy Spirit!" and walk off without providing so much as a coat or a cup of soup—where does that get you? Isn't it obvious that God-talk without God-acts is outrageous nonsense?

The love of our neighbor is the litmus test for our love of God. The same is true of our deeds. They are proof of the authenticity of our words. To "believe," to "follow Jesus," to "understand" all suggest an element of active commitment that flows into deeds. *Justice is love.* This is the essence of what Jesus came to teach. The principle for every act and attitude is love of God and our neighbor. Jesus said,

> "You shall love the LORD your God with all your heart, with all your soul, and with all your mind." This is the first and great commandment. And the second is like it: "You shall love your neighbor as yourself." On these two commandments hang all the Law and the Prophets. (Matt. 22:37–40 NKJV)

Though the new language on the lips of Christians in the New Testament was the language of love, it was more than just a language. It was something with power, something that prompted action. Early Christians considered themselves members of the same family, true brothers and sisters. Tertullian, an early Christian, noted what unbelievers said about the Christians: "It is our care for the helpless, our practice of loving-kindness, that brands us in the eyes of many of our opponents. 'Only look,' they say, 'look how they love one another!' Thus had this saying become a fact: 'Hereby shall all men know that ye are my disciples, if ye have love one to another.'"

Love is expressed through justice for the oppressed.

If justice burns in your bones, that little voice is probably yelling at full volume now. And why would it not burn in you? Our God is certainly a God of justice, and we are his people. We who call ourselves Christ-followers are not only encouraged to rise up and do something—anything to make a difference—we are compelled. Compelled by love.

ARE WE A PEOPLE OF JUSTICE?

The United States was built on the concept of justice. That little phrase "innocent until proven guilty" is a great example of this. I'm sure you can come up with a few other phrases that echo with similar intent—phrases like "with liberty and justice for all" and "all men are created equal."

Children have a built-in system of justice. I can't tell you the number of times my seven-year-old, Gideon, has told me, "That's not fair!" It's his mantra. Though he's not always right, he certainly has a sense that equality exists ... and that he's not always a recipient of that equality.

The civil rights movement was a movement about justice. People were being treated unfairly simply because of the color of their skin. People who listened to that internal voice crying out for justice wouldn't let this evil go unnoticed. One of the most motivating speeches of our time, by the Reverend Dr. Martin Luther King Jr., will echo in the hearts of men and women until the next millennia:

> I have a dream that one day this nation will rise up and live out the true meaning of its creed: "We hold these truths to be self-evident, that all men are created equal."
>
> I have a dream that one day on the red hills of Georgia, the sons of former slaves and the sons of former slave owners will be able to sit down together at the table of brotherhood.
>
> I have a dream that one day even the state of Mississippi, a state sweltering with the heat of injustice, sweltering with the heat of oppression, will be transformed into an oasis of freedom and justice.
>
> I have a dream that my four little children will one day live in a nation where they will not be judged by the color of their skin but by the content of their character.
>
> I have a dream today![3]

I'm both inspired and heartbroken by this speech. The inspiration is obvious—who of us wouldn't want a world where all men and women are indeed treated as equals? But there is a palpable sense of heartbreak in Dr. King's use of the word *dream*. A dream is something that has not yet moved from the realm of a great idea into the reality of our daily lives. Dr. King's vision is a dream because we haven't made it happen yet. Sure, we've made progress, most notably in the civil rights arena. Yet there is much distance yet to travel along the path to justice.

I have a dream too, that God's justice will rule and reign over all of this green earth. I have a dream of a world where no one has to live in extreme poverty, where slavery isn't in the hearts of people, where there is no such word as *orphan*. I have a dream that God's people will wake up and recognize who they truly are in Christ—people God can use to set the captives free.

Yeah, I have a dream. But it doesn't have to remain a dream.

WHAT KIND OF GOSPEL DID JESUS COME TO BRING?

Jesus believed in the sanctity of human life. He believed that each person living on planet Earth had the right to be free, to live with dignity, to be safe, to receive care for their sickness or disease, and to be loved by the community.

This is the good news Jesus came to deliver—the good news of God's intervention to help his people. Jesus didn't simply call people to repentance and then walk away, his work complete. No, he walked among the people. He touched them. He healed them. He called them to a better way of living and revealed himself as the hope of the poor.

We, as Christ-followers, are called to continue the work Jesus began. What does this mean? It means we have to embody the good news. It means we have to do all we can to end poverty, to feed the hungry, and to find homes for the homeless. It means we have to listen to that inner voice crying for justice and act on it.

UNIVERSAL DECLARATION OF HUMAN RIGHTS

The secular world recognizes that human life has value regardless of race, physical condition, or socioeconomic status. In 1948, the United Nations adopted and announced a "Universal Declaration of Human Rights" that is recognized worldwide. Here's how it begins:

> Whereas recognition of the inherent dignity and of the equal and inalienable rights of all members of the human family is the foundation of freedom, justice and peace in the world,
>
> Whereas disregard and contempt for human rights have resulted in barbarous acts which have outraged the conscience of mankind, and the advent of a world in which human beings shall enjoy freedom of speech and belief and freedom from fear and want has been proclaimed as the highest aspiration of the common people.[4]

The text of the Universal Declaration of Human Rights is composed of thirty articles representing agreement from many nations. This document was written as a statement of what it means to live morally in relation to other human beings. It was not written from a particular religious mind-set. It simply has to do with what people almost universally agree are inalienable rights. They fall into three major categories:

The rights to life and the nonviolability of a person. These rights are aimed at keeping the integrity of the individual.

Civil and political rights. These rights include "freedom of expression and assembly, the right to a public hearing by an impartial tribunal, and rights to take part in government and public activities."

Socioeconomic rights. This category of rights ensures that the conditions exist for every person to realize "a dignified material and spiritual existence."

If the secular world can recognize the individual rights of street kids, orphans, widows, AIDS patients, and other marginalized members of society, how much more then should we who believe the good news Jesus Christ came to bring not only recognize these rights but fight for them?

MOTHER TERESA

Mother Teresa fought for justice, not because she was compelled by the words in the Universal Declaration of Human Rights, but because she saw the image of God in the lepers, the crippled, and the street urchins she served. Why do we have a difficult time seeing God in the eyes of the poor? Perhaps because for some of us it's easier to see God in the beautiful, the dazzling, and the successful. But Jesus didn't say, "As you've done it unto the *best* of these, you've done it to me." It's the "least of these" whom Jesus identified with.

Mother Teresa understood this on a deep level. Her commitment and communion with Christ taught her what was truly important on this earth. She welcomed every day with a sense of excitement and anticipation because each day was another opportunity to find Jesus in the lives of the poor. "I try to give to the poor people for love what the rich could get for money," she once said. "No, I wouldn't touch a leper for a thousand pounds; yet I willingly cure him for the love of God."

When we see the world through God's eyes, we see a different picture than when we look only through our own eyes. We see the hard reality of injustice. We see people being abandoned and violated. And we see a world crying out for the realization of that dream of equality. This was how Mother Teresa viewed the world. She saw a humanity that was broken because of poverty and disease—a humanity that ached to know the love of Jesus. She extended grace and mercy to those who were most in need of it. She met people—people created in the image of God—right where they were, in the most disparaging of circumstances. Mother Teresa was compelled to serve the needs of the poor, because that is exactly what God would do. This is the work of justice.

> When a poor person dies of hunger, it has not happened
> because God did not take care of him or her. It has hap-
> pened because neither you nor I wanted to give that

person what he or she needed. We have refused to be instruments of love in the hands of God to give the poor a piece of bread, to offer them a dress with which to ward off the cold. It has happened because we did not recognize Christ when, once more, he appeared under the guise of pain, identified with a man numb from the cold, dying of hunger, when he came in a lonely human being, in a lost child in search of a home.[5]

Are you tired? Worn out? Burned out on religion? Come to me. Get away with me and you'll recover your life. I'll show you how to take a real rest. Walk with me and work with me—watch how I do it. Learn the unforced rhythms of grace. I won't lay anything heavy or ill-fitting on you. Keep company with me and you'll learn to live freely and lightly.

—Matthew 11:28–30

THE MOST IMPORTANT THINGS

MAKE A MENTAL list of the top five things that matter most to you. I'll give you a moment …

Got it? Let me see if I can guess some of the things on that list. Family? Friends? Your relationship with God? Maybe safety or security? These are all good things. God-honoring things. My list is probably a lot like yours. But here's a million-dollar question: Do our lists match God's?

I wonder if the 5,500 Africans dying every day from preventable and treatable diseases are at the top of his list?[1] What about the 640,000 children under age fifteen who were newly infected with HIV in 2006, bringing the total number of children living with HIV to 2.2 million?[2] What about the:

- 28 million children who die from curable diseases each year?
- 17 million children who die from malnutrition and starvation each year?
- 33 percent of the world's population that is malnourished?
- 20 percent of the world's population that has no access to safe water?
- 10 million children who are involved in the sex industry?
- 100 million children who live on the streets?
- 200 million child laborers?[3]

Are these people on God's list of "What Matters Most"?

Surely they are. And yet we respond, "Well, God is big enough to include them on his list. But I'm not God. Certainly he doesn't expect me to have the same sort of list. I mean, I have so many demands on my time. So many things fill my days and my mind. Good things, most of them."

Yes, we are busy. We have lots of demands on our time. And we can't, on our own, solve these bigger-than-life problems. But we can use our influence in many difference-making ways. We can be advocates. We can care. We can pray. We can recruit others. We can act. But before we do any of those things, we need to add these people to our "What Matters Most" list.

THE LEAST OF THESE

The teaching in Matthew 25 occurred only two days before Jesus was handed over to the authorities to be crucified. The specific language Jesus used and the fact that this was so close to his death reveal the importance of the passage. Let's look at it again:

> When he finally arrives, blazing in beauty and all his angels with him, the Son of Man will take his place on his glorious throne. Then all the nations will be arranged before him and he will sort the people out, much as a shepherd sorts out sheep and goats, putting sheep to his right and goats to his left.
>
> Then the King will say to those on his right, "Enter, you who are blessed by my Father! Take what's coming to you in this kingdom. It's been ready for you since the world's foundation. And here's why:
>
> I was hungry and you fed me,
>
> I was thirsty and you gave me a drink,
>
> I was homeless and you gave me a room,
>
> I was shivering and you gave me clothes,
>
> I was sick and you stopped to visit,
>
> I was in prison and you came to me."
>
> Then those "sheep" are going to say, "Master, what are you talking about? When did we ever see you hungry and feed you, thirsty and give you a drink? And when did we ever see you sick or in prison and come to you?" Then

the King will say, "I'm telling the solemn truth: Whenever you did one of these things to someone overlooked or ignored, that was me—you did it to me." (Matt. 25:31–40)

Acting out of mercy, giving a cup of cold water to a thirsty child, visiting the orphan, giving hope and life to someone suffering from AIDS—these are the things at the top of God's priority list. Jesus is interested in what we're doing with our compassion and acts of mercy. He doesn't care about how religious we appear. If our Christian faith doesn't manifest into something that helps the life of another human being, it doesn't mean squat to him.

I am inspired by the life of Oscar Schindler every time I watch the movie *Schindler's List*. I'll never forget the final scene when he is on his knees crying out in agony because he realizes he could have done more—he could have saved more lives. Though Schindler was known to be a swindler and war profiteer, he spent millions of dollars out of his own pocket to protect the Jews. He risked his life to save theirs. He bribed the Nazis; he created jobs in his factory for the sick so they wouldn't be sent to Auschwitz. Oscar Schindler recognized that he had been given influence, resources, and the ability to make a difference in what seemed like a hopeless situation. The moment he stepped out and trusted God to help him save lives, God met him and did more than he could have ever dreamed. More than twelve hundred people were kept from the gas chambers because of his actions.

What if you knew your actions could prevent even one death?

What if you knew you had the influence, resources, and ability to make a difference in what seemed like a hopeless situation? Would you act? Would you be like Oscar Schindler, or would you remain silent?

"NEUTRALITY HELPS THE OPPRESSOR"

Far too many of us take the easy route, the path of least resistance. The path of doing nothing. I don't think this is because we're evil, or because we want to see harm come to others; it's just easier. Safer. But is silence really "safe"? Author and Holocaust survivor Elie Wiesel wrote, "I swore never to be silent whenever and wherever human beings endure suffering and humiliation. We must always take sides. Neutrality helps the oppressor, never the victim. Silence encourages the tormentor, never the tormented."[4]

Listen, I know this isn't the easiest thing to hear. I could have filled this book with platitudes and niceties about "doing the best we can" and proclaiming "everything will be okay because God is full of grace and forgives our hard hearts," but that would be a waste of paper. A waste of your precious time. And it would be dishonest.

This is the uncomfortable "rub" we bump into in Matthew 25. There are a few ways we can respond to this passage. We can be offended by it, we can hope it's just plain wrong, or we can allow it to spray our faces with the icy water of truth. Is God really *that* passionate about the poor and the needy?

I think you and I both know the answer to that.

LIVING BIGGER THAN YOURSELF

How do you want to be remembered? What would you want other people to say about how you lived your life? Go ahead; think about it. What would be written in your obituary? That you were a good person? That you worked hard? That you were a successful businessman or woman? What would it say about the impact you had on others?

For many Americans, life is defined essentially by our "stuff." By the house we live in and by the car we drive. By the diploma we hang on the wall and the size of our bank account. But we weren't created so we could simply amass wealth and influence. We were created for something more. To live for something bigger than ourselves.

Solomon wrestled with this very issue. Though he had everything this world could offer him, he found himself still wanting. It wasn't enough. He wasn't satisfied. He wrote, "He [God] has made everything beautiful in its time. He has also set eternity in the hearts of men; yet they cannot fathom what God has done from beginning to end" (Eccl. 3:11 NIV).

The story of the rich young ruler adds further insight into this issue. Before we talk about the story, I want to emphasize that I don't think you have to sell everything you own and give it to the poor in order to have favor with Jesus. I believe the point of this story is a much simpler truth: Jesus knew the man cared more about his earthly possessions than he did about following Jesus, and the only way to get him to see this was to offer a dramatic challenge.

As Jesus started on his way, a man ran up to him and fell on his knees before him. "Good teacher," he asked, "what must I do to inherit eternal life?"

"Why do you call me good?" Jesus answered. "No one is good—except God alone. You know the commandments: 'Do not murder, do not commit adultery, do not steal, do not give false testimony, do not defraud, honor your father and mother.'"

"Teacher," he declared, "all these I have kept since I was a boy."

Jesus looked at him and loved him. "One thing you lack," he said. "Go, sell everything you have and give to the poor, and you will have treasure in heaven. Then come, follow me."

At this the man's face fell. He went away sad, because he had great wealth. (Mark 10:17–22 NIV)

Jesus told the man what his heart was searching for, but the man just wasn't ready to receive it. He wasn't ready to live for something bigger than himself. I often wonder what this man's life would have looked like if he had accepted Jesus' invitation. "Follow me," Jesus had offered. What an invitation. This man could have walked the earth alongside the Creator of the universe. He could have witnessed miracles. And he could have learned what it meant to follow God from God himself. Instead, he just turned and walked away, a victim of his own selfishness, of his inability to live a truly big life, not as calculated by dollars and cents, but as calculated by the incalculable impact he could have had on the lives of others.

If we live for something bigger than ourselves, we'll never be cheated. We'll never lose out; we will always be given more than our wildest dreams.

How Will Our Generation Be Remembered?

I had an epiphany at the Denver U2 "How to Dismantle an Atomic Bomb" concert. Bono was talking about this very issue. "What does it mean to live a life of significance? How will we be remembered?"

He talked about how our generation would be remembered. The '60s will always be remembered for the civil rights movement. In the '80s we defeated communism. But what will our generation be remembered for? YouTube? MySpace? Reality television? Wouldn't it be better if we could be known for defeating poverty?

Bono suggested that this is an attainable goal. Not the defeat of all poverty of course, but extreme poverty—the kind of poverty where people die needlessly from things like AIDS and malaria. In his book *The End of Poverty*, Jeffrey Sachs claimed that if all good people worked together and did something to be involved, extreme poverty could be eliminated by the year 2025.[5]

Hundred of thousands, even millions of lives could be saved because of our actions. Now that's living for something bigger than ourselves. As Bono said,

We are the first generation that can look extreme and stupid poverty in the eye, look across the water to Africa and
elsewhere and say this and mean it: we have the cash, we
have the drugs, we have the science—but do we have the
will? Do we have the will to make poverty history? Some
say we can't afford to. I say we can't afford not to.[6]

One day the history books will be written about us—what we
did and what we didn't do. We're writing that history today. But
how will it read? Will the books say, "This was a generation that
took the sanctity of human life issue seriously. This was a generation that lived out the Christian message by caring for the poor,
saving the lives of the innocent, and eradicating extreme poverty."
Or will those pages be filled with pictures of our opulence, evidence of our selfishness?

How do you want to be remembered?

Who needs a doctor: the healthy or the sick? Go figure out what this Scripture means: "I'm after mercy, not religion." I'm here to invite outsiders, not coddle insiders.

—Matthew 9:12

9

SNAPSHOTS
OF HOPE

IN THE PREVIOUS chapter, I encouraged you to think about
what's really important in this life. I challenged you to live bigger
than yourself. So, how are you feeling about that? Excited?
Hopeful? Frightened? Overwhelmed? Maybe you're thinking, *I
like the idea, but I don't have anything to offer. I'm just an ordinary
person living an ordinary life.* Ah, but you *do* have something to
offer. This chapter is all about ordinary people—people like you
and me—and what they've done to make a difference.

Too often, we sit on the sidelines, waiting for some grand sign from God that we're supposed to get into the game. When that lightning doesn't strike, we shrug our shoulders and think, *I guess God doesn't need me here.* Meanwhile, as we sit in our recliners, drumming our fingers and waiting for that burning-bush experience, people all around the world are crying out for help. Crying out for a miracle. Maybe you don't have something so grand as an answer for their poverty or cure for their disease. But you can offer them something else, something that is just as much of a miracle: hope.

But first, we have to get up out of the chair. When we decide to move, our eyes are suddenly opened. It doesn't take a burning-bush experience to see Jesus in the eyes of those suffering from HIV/AIDS in Africa. With every small step, our faith comes alive, and things we thought were impossible start to happen. I'm going to share just four stories that all began with small steps. These are stories of ordinary people. Ordinary people who got out of their ordinary chairs and followed our extraordinary God to give hope to the hopeless. Any one of these stories could be your story.

RESCUING THE ABANDONED

Robyn and Gerry Richter had been keeping an eye on a Swazi mother who was pregnant and didn't want the baby. One fateful day a friend came to them with the disturbing news that this mother had gone into a hut pregnant, and come out no longer pregnant, but also childless. They raced into the hut, but found no baby. When they walked outside, they came upon a fresh pile of dirt. They quickly dug through the dirt and found the baby alive with the umbilical cord still attached.

This was just one of more than a hundred babies Robyn and Gerry have rescued since they began their ministry. In their own words, here's how their story began:

> In August 1992, an abandoned, four-month-old boy found his way into our home. He was extremely malnourished, neglected, and deprived. He weighed only 3.4 kgs (7.5 lbs)! As I nursed him back to life, he found a very special place in our hearts and lives. When he was well and gaining weight and the threat of death had been removed from his life, we tried desperately to find a good family to take him in, as at this point we had three of our own children and a foster son to care for.
>
> When we realized that there was nowhere else for him to go, we decided to adopt him as our own son. In November 1993, another little abandoned boy found his way into our home. This one was twelve months old and had been physically abused, also suffering from neglect and kwashiorkor (extreme lack of protein in the diet). After nursing him back to health, we realized that there was nowhere for him to go, and so we adopted him as well.
>
> It was due to this lack that we looked into the matter and found that very little help was being given to the

abandoned or unwanted babies. In Swaziland, there is no Children's Act to protect the child. Children are not at the top of the priority list, and so very little was being done to accommodate them.

The Swazi government is gradually becoming more aware of the plight of abused or abandoned babies, and something is starting to be done about the problem. But change takes time, and for some children time is running out. When we realized this, we made a decision to help these children wherever we could. It was out of this need that ABC Ministry was born.

ABC's vision is to love and care for abandoned babies and give them the chance to bond to a mother figure in the early months of their lives. The babies they are unable to return to their families or place into adoptive homes remain a part of the ABC Ministry Home until the age of three or four. Then they're moved to permanent foster homes in the Bulembu Village of Hope Orphan Village, where they can be raised to adulthood under the love and care of foster parents.

A PAIR OF SHOES

Natasha Koryakina is a second-year university student in Russia, majoring in foreign languages. She looks like any happy normal Russian young woman, and you might guess she comes from a happy normal home. You'd be guessing wrong. Her happiness isn't the product of a wonderful family life. In fact, her past is marked by pain, abandonment, and abuse. So where did she find her smile? It was a gift handed to her by a man named George Steiner. "I still remember how George put shoes on my feet when I was at Neya orphanage," says Natasha. "It was me, Natasha Chekina and another boy from my class. We still talk about it every time we get together. That small, little moment changed our lives in a profound way."

In the ten years that have passed since that "small, little moment," Natasha graduated from one of the worst orphanages in the Kostroma region and entered a tech school in Kostroma. She eventually got plugged in to the Ministry Center, a local program sponsored by Children's HopeChest (www.hopechest.org), and graduated from her tech school with honors before being accepted to Kostroma State University, a truly rare accomplishment (less than 1 percent of orphans reach this milestone). Natasha is a straight-A student, a translator for many Christian teams that visit Russia, a mentor for two orphan girls, and just an amazing person.

The odds were against Natasha. Most girls living in Russian orphanages are forced to leave when they turn fifteen or sixteen. Within two years of their release, 15 percent commit suicide and 60 percent end up as prostitutes.

But when George Steiner put those shoes on her feet, he tipped the scale just enough with his encouragement and compassion to help her rise above the statistics. His small act helped her to believe in herself. Recently, Natasha also reconciled with her mother, whose neglect and alcohol addiction resulted in Natasha's being sent to the orphanage many years ago.

Natasha will never forget George ... a tall man in a big hat. All he did was give her shoes. But God used those shoes to help Natasha walk into a wonderful, new hope-filled life.

A GIRL NAMED BUSI

Busiswewe (Busi for short) was six years old when she was discovered in a Swaziland hospital by visiting missionaries. She had been admitted after suffering third-degree burns on more than 40 percent of her body. The scar tissue fused her limbs, leaving her almost immobile, and she was in need of extensive skin grafting and reconstruction. To add to the tragedy, both her parents died of AIDS while she was in the hospital. She could easily have become yet another statistic—another abandoned child left to die alone. And she might have, except for a man named Claude. This is Claude's story:

> The first time I saw Busi was in July of 2005 at a government hospital in Bubane, Swaziland, in the ward where they take care of abandoned infants. I was visiting with the other orphaned children when Busi came into the room having undressed for her bath. There were no clothes to hide her awful burn scars that went from her neck to her thighs. I could even see the way the flames must have wrapped around her arm. I later learned her

clothes had caught on fire while she was cooking over an open flame. She still had open wounds, and she was stuck in a forward lean, about 75 degrees, because her upper legs were fused with scar tissue to her torso.

I completely lost it. A fatherly concern for her and an urgent need to seek proper care for her came over me. As I began to ask questions, I was initially brushed aside with comments like "She has a family," and "She's no concern of yours; don't get involved." After much prodding, I finally learned the truth: both her parents had died while she was at the hospital, probably from AIDS, although the death certificates just stated the secondary disease symptoms because of the cultural shame over this STD. Busi, along with the other abandoned children, was now in the care of the ward. She was surviving, but she was still in no condition to consider attending school.

Busi had no caregiver, no plan for treatment. The hospital nurses would change her dressings every other day, but even now, a year later, it was still a very painful process. Her accident had occurred in November of 2004, but she was taken out of the hospital, before her wounds had healed, by her father, due to a conflict between his ancestral worship and the hospital's modern medicine. Sometime in January or February of 2005, she was returned to the hospital by her mother, who could no longer stand to see her suffering. In May of that year, both Busi's parents died within the same week. Even so, as I inquired about her care, the government workers would commit to helping in any way possible, and then, in the same breath, throw up obstacles about seeking specialized care out-of-country.

Then, out of the blue, an advocate came up and said to me, "Claude, you must drive to the capital city today; you must see the magistrate." It was one of those situations where you don't ask questions, but simply follow through on the command in trust and wonder. The magistrate, in turn, said, "I have become aware of your situation. I am also a Christian and share your concern for the children. You are trying to do the right thing, and no one should stand in your way. This is what I would like to do: even though you are technically too young, and you have not spent the required year of custodial care, if you are willing to, I am ready to give Busi totally into your care. I am willing to sign the necessary paperwork right now to make her wholly yours; she will be your child to seek whatever care you see fit for her, and no one will be able to say otherwise because she is yours." In amazement, I quickly agreed, and within twenty minutes I had in hand a document that normally takes over a year (not to mention a lot of red tape) to achieve.

Within a week, I had Busi in to see a top-quality plastic surgeon, a burn specialist, at the government hospital over the border in Praetoria, South Africa. This doctor was a friend, and he had agreed to do the surgery for free. After the corrective surgery and a month in recuperation and growing new skin, it was time to seek enrollment in a local school.

Against all odds, doors opened for Claude to enroll Busi in one of the best schools available. And the miracles continued. Though Swaziland law has no allowance for foreigners adopting the orphans in their country, through a series of miraculous events, Claude and his wife, Mary, were able to adopt the now nine-year-old Busi as their daughter.

Known By Name

My friend Seth Barnes told me an incredible story of young people who are doing something to make a difference in India. Imagine an orphanage outside Delhi, India, where 370 orphans live on seven cents a day. Overcrowded conditions mean that several children share each metal, mattress-less bunk. Precious drinking water is ferried in by trucks, but there is none to waste on dirty fingers—dirty fingers that hungrily scoop rice into eager mouths whenever it is offered. Soap is a luxury.

The children suffer from a boil that eats away at their skin, but the antibiotics needed to cure the disease cost more than the rice needed to keep the children alive. They also suffer from scabies and lice, which are accepted as a normal part of an orphan's existence. Yet the children never complain. At least they have a roof over their heads, unlike many of their friends left behind in Delhi's leper colonies or slums.

"Who supports this orphanage?" Seth asked Alli, a young volunteer.

"We do," she said. "Our teams from the U.S. feed the children and clean their scabies. If we aren't there to buy rice when it runs out, the kids go hungry. In the summer, the heat gets up to over one hundred and twenty-five degrees, and there is never enough water. It gets so hot they can't sleep at night. In the winter it is just as bad. There are not enough blankets for every child, so they huddle like puppies in a pile on the concrete floor, surviving on each other's body heat."

Alli told Seth about a team member named Allen who had developed a special relationship with little Suraj-john at the orphanage. Allen had told her what it was like to say good-bye to him: "When it came time to leave, he gave me a big hug and looked at me intently and said, 'Don't forget me, Allen Uncle. I am Suraj-john. Don't forget me when you leave. I know your name. Your name is Allen Uncle. I love you, Allen Uncle. My name is Suraj-john.'"

That's all that matters to these kids. That's all that matters to these who have no father and no mother and no human comfort. That we remember their names. Not that we remember to buy rice for them or remember to bring soccer balls to them. It's that we remember their names: Suraj-john, Pooja, Radha, Tannu. But we want to do more than remember their names.

I've heard stories of the prayers of these children. Three to five times a day, they drop to their knees on the concrete floor. Eyes tightly closed and hands clasped under their chins, they cry out to God. But their prayers might surprise you. Though they have learned to rely on God for all their needs and sometimes ask him to supply those needs, most of their prayers are filled with sentences like these: "God, please bless Alli Auntie. God, please be with Allen Uncle."

They remember *our* names.

And because a few twentysomethings from America remember theirs, they have hope.

THE COMPELLING NATURE OF COMPASSION

What compels a family living a comfortable life to move into a slum, adopt an orphan, and build a church? What prompts a successful businessman to leave his job and start a nonprofit organization to provide food and education to otherwise hopeless orphans? What drives a young, corporate real estate executive to cash in his investments so he can serve the poor of the world? Or a schoolmaster to give up his living room for a classroom, feed his students from his own kitchen, and build a five-room school with his own hands? Or a sickly widow living in a mud hut with a dirt floor to take in more than twenty hungry, homeless orphans?

Compassion. Love. A heart like Christ's. And eyes that can see Jesus in "the least of these." That's what gets these people out of their chairs. These people aren't millionaires. They aren't rock stars.

They're just ordinary people who understand the importance of bringing hope to the hopeless.

As Christ-followers, we're not only called to preach the good news, we're called to embody it with our very lives. This is no easy task. We face a powerful enemy intent on destroying all that is good.

> The thief comes only to steal and kill and destroy; I came that they may have life, and have it abundantly.
>
> I am the good shepherd; the good shepherd lays down His life for the sheep.
>
> He who is a hired hand, and not a shepherd, who is not the owner of the sheep, sees the wolf coming, and leaves the sheep and flees, and the wolf snatches them and scatters them.
>
> He flees because he is a hired hand and is not concerned about the sheep.
>
> I am the good shepherd, and I know My own and My own know Me. (John 10:10–14 NASB)

I believe we stand as shepherds underneath the leadership of the Good Shepherd. We are commanded to take care of his sheep. But many flocks—like the millions suffering from HIV/AIDS in Africa—have been left unattended, and the thief has stolen and killed and destroyed lives. The world is crying out for more shepherds.

Sometimes I get discouraged when I think of the magnitude of need in our world and then see how many Christ-followers remain stuck to their chairs. I am heartbroken when I hear the roaring silence of a church unwilling to speak up for the voiceless masses. In times like these I feel defeated. I begin to form that word *impossible* with my lips. But before I speak it, God reminds me of his strength and ability to make the impossible possible.

Then he took me back to the riverbank. While sitting on the bank, I noticed a lot of trees on both sides of the river. He told me, "This water flows east, descends to the Arabah and then into the sea, the sea of stagnant waters. When it empties into those waters, the sea will become fresh. Wherever the river flows, life will flourish—great schools of fish—because the river is turning the salt sea into fresh water. Where the river flows, life abounds. Fishermen will stand shoulder to shoulder along the shore from En-gedi all the way north to En-eglaim, casting their nets. The sea will teem with fish of all kinds, like the fish of the Great Mediterranean.

"The swamps and marshes won't become fresh. They'll stay salty.

"But the river itself, on both banks, will grow fruit trees of all kinds. Their leaves won't wither, the fruit won't fail. Every month they'll bear fresh fruit because the river from the Sanctuary flows to them. Their fruit will be for food and their leaves for healing." (Ezek. 47:6–12)

Everything lives where the river flows! It doesn't matter how dead, how lifeless, how hopeless, or how impossible. It doesn't matter how difficult things might be, how hopeless the situation might seem, or how insignificant we might feel about making a difference. If we rely on God's power to make dead things come to life, we will live what Jesus lived and see what Jesus saw.

There is hope for those suffering from HIV/AIDS in Africa. There is hope for all who suffer from hopelessness. And that hope is you.

And me.

Are you ready to get out of that chair? Then you're ready for the next chapter.

For whoever wants to save his life will lose it, but whoever loses his life for me will find it. What good will it be for a man if he gains the whole world, yet forfeits his soul? Or what can a man give in exchange for his soul? For the Son of Man is going to come in his Father's glory with his angels, and then he will reward each person according to what he has done. I tell you the truth, some who are standing here will not taste death before they see the Son of Man coming in his kingdom.

—**Matthew 16:25–28** NIV

10

HOW TO
BLEED

THE SUBTITLE OF this book is "Living a Faith That Bleeds."
Perhaps that image is a bit disturbing to you. *A faith that bleeds? I
don't want to bleed,* you might think. I don't imagine any of us likes
the idea of bleeding, but as Christ-followers, we can't deny the significance of blood. The thing is, even in our churches we tend to
sidestep this image. We have little problem stating that "Jesus died
for our sins" because "death" is an existential concept we can safely
wrestle with. But to say, "Jesus *bled* and died for our sins," now
that's a little tougher to handle. That little word *bled* puts flesh on

Jesus and then tears at that flesh in an uncomfortably visceral way. During Communion we mention Jesus' shed blood, but we see it only as a symbol. After all, that's only grape juice or wine in the cup, right?

Simply stated, we're uncomfortable with blood. Talking about it makes us queasy. Oh, sure, some of us can watch Tarantino's latest film without a single wince, but that's different—that's not real blood. That's not your blood. That's not mine.

When we think of blood, we think of injury. Of someone in need. Perhaps of sacrifice. But there's something else we ought to think of—we ought to think of life. Blood *is* life. Without it, we are nothing.

So what is this "faith that bleeds"? Yes, it's a faith that requires sacrifice. But more than that, it's a faith that brings *life*.

Living the Red Letters life is living a transformed life—a life where the needs of the poor and the diseased rank high on your "what's important" list.

In the pages that follow, I'm going to offer you plenty to think about. I'm going to tell you about the "Five for 50" campaign—a program you can ease into beginning today that will make an immediate and dramatic difference in the lives of HIV/AIDS sufferers in Africa. And I'm going to point you toward other ways you can make a difference.

Now I know it's possible you still may be unsure about all of this—perhaps you're a little overwhelmed. I don't expect all of you to pack your bags for Africa after you set this book on the table. (Although if that's what God calls you to do, then do it!) Most of you will want to think and pray about your next step. You'll want to talk with friends or family. Do whatever you need to do … just find a way to get up out of that chair.

These Red Letter words ought to help: "Whenever you did one of these things to someone overlooked or ignored, that was me—you did it to me" (Matt. 25:40).

THE NEXT STEP

I've been promising specific ways you can change the world. Your involvement in any one of the programs I'm about to present could mean the difference between life and death for one or a dozen or a hundred people. Taking a step of faith can rescue someone from poverty, provide life-saving medicine for a person suffering from AIDS, or offer an educational opportunity otherwise unavailable to a school-age child.

So here we go. Following is a list of ways you can be involved in different causes and different areas of need. The choice is yours. But do something.

PRAY DAILY

Before you do anything else, make a commitment to pray daily for the people affected by the HIV/AIDS pandemic and all the people of the world who suffer from poverty and hopelessness. Come up with your own prayer, or use ones I've included below.

Here's how I often pray:

Almighty and most merciful God, we remember before you all poor and neglected persons: the homeless and the destitute, the old and the sick, and all who have none to care for them. Help us to heal those who are broken in body or spirit, and to turn their sorrow into joy. Grant this, Father, for the love of your Son, Jesus Christ our Lord, who for our sake became poor. Amen.

And here is a wonderfully apt prayer from Saint Francis of Assisi:

Lord, make me an instrument of Thy peace;

where there is hatred, let me sow love;

where there is injury, pardon;

where there is doubt, faith;

where there is despair, hope;

where there is darkness, light;

and where there is sadness, joy.

O Divine Master,

grant that I may not so much seek to be consoled as to console;

to be understood, as to understand;

to be loved, as to love;

for it is in giving that we receive,

it is in pardoning that we are pardoned,

and it is in dying that we are born to eternal life.

Amen.

FIVE FOR 50

What is Five for 50? It's a comprehensive plan to bring Christians from all across the globe together in solidarity with the soon-to-be fifty million people living with HIV. There are five "steps" to this program, each of them requiring just a little bit more sacrifice than the previous. Even if you're not sure how far you can follow through with this program, *every* step is important and *every* step makes a difference. Here's how it works.

The steps of Five for 50 are as follows:

Give five minutes a day to pray for those suffering from HIV/AIDS.

Give five hours a week to fast for those suffering from HIV/AIDS.

Give five dollars a month to the Five for 50 Fund to support worthy causes.

Give five days a year to travel overseas to help alleviate poverty and suffering.

Give five people an opportunity to join you on your journey.

STEP 1: GIVE FIVE MINUTES A DAY TO PRAY FOR THOSE SUFFERING FROM HIV/AIDS.

"It is written," he said to them, "'My house will be called a house of prayer'" (Matt. 21:13 NIV).

"If you believe, you will receive whatever you ask for in prayer" (Matt. 21:22 NIV).

Jesus built his ministry on a foundation of prayer. That's how we want to build the Five for 50 ministry as well. Take five minutes each day to pray for the fifty million people infected with HIV, and stand in solidarity with them.

How are you going to find time to do this? Cut five minutes out of your ICQ or Instant Messenger chatting time; get up five minutes early; go to bed five minutes later; surf the Net five minutes less. There are hundreds of ways to pull this off.

During this period of time, remember the suffering of our brothers and sisters. The places that have the highest rates of HIV in the world are Africa, India, China, and Russia. Lift these people up in prayer for things such as:

- Easing their suffering
- Strengthening their bodies
- Finding access to proper medication and medical care
- Dignity in illness
- Overcoming societal stigmas
- Bringing more workers to the field

If you like to follow a more systematic form of prayer, consider the daily office. There are plenty of books available that explain this monastic tradition, or you can find more information online at sites such as www.northumbriacommunity.org. There you will find prayers for the morning, midday, and evening.

Perhaps some thoughts are already floating around in your spirit about how you might want to pray for those suffering from

HIV/AIDS. Go ahead and write those down in the space follow-ing this paragraph. Then refer back to this page as you build your plan for five minutes of prayer a day.

STEP 2: GIVE FIVE HOURS A WEEK TO FAST FOR THOSE SUFFERING FROM HIV/AIDS.

Don't be afraid of this step—you can go without food for five hours. If you've never fasted before, I would suggest you find and read a book by Elmer Towns called *The Beginner's Guide to Fasting.*

The idea behind the Five for 50 fast is to abstain from food for just five hours, and to remember during those five hours the mil-lions of people who live in poverty and may not eat for days at a time. Fasts are made more powerful when they're combined with prayer. Our suggestion of five hours is merely a starting place. As you learn this spiritual act of faith, you will be able to increase the fasting time to a day, and then perhaps even longer.

To start, I recommend fasting between breakfast and dinner—skipping lunch while you're at work. But don't work during this lunch time. Spend your lunch hour in prayer or in some other action step that exemplifies Red Letter living. With each hunger pang or belly growl, pray for those whose daily diet barely fills their little hands—let alone their stomachs.

STEP 3: GIVE FIVE DOLLARS A MONTH TO THE FIVE FOR 50 FUND OR OTHER WORTHY CAUSES.

As you already know, I am a big fan of Starbucks. Perhaps you are too. But whether you head to a national chain or the independent shop around the corner, you're bound to spend at least five dollars every time you collect that steaming cup from the happy barista. Why not trade one of your lattes to help save a life or two? It's not so much to ask. Not a coffee drinker? I'm sure you can find some way to come up with five dollars a month to help make a difference.

There are literally thousands of great organizations where you could send that money. If you already have one in mind, write a check or set up an automatic withdrawal and give, give, give. (Five dollars a month is just a starting suggestion; the sky's the limit.) If you don't know where to send your money, consider the Five for 50 Fund. The money donated to this fund will be invested in only the most effective responses to HIV/AIDS.

As you think about giving, don't forget Jesus' words: "For where your treasure is, there your heart will be also" (Luke 12:34 NIV).

Go to www.fivefor50.com for a complete list of online giving options and links to the supported organizations.

STEP 4: GIVE FIVE DAYS A YEAR TO TRAVEL OVERSEAS
TO HELP ALLEVIATE POVERTY AND SUFFERING.

After you've invested yourself in the three steps above, I want you to think about moving in a direction that will change your life forever. Give five days of your life to take a trip into Africa or another nation where people are hungry for the hope you can bring.

A number of different organizations can arrange a trip for you, some of which are included in the resources to follow. Most prepare a detailed plan, including all ground transportation and translators, and even offer options for side trips, so all you have to do is raise the funds and then show up at the airport. I know this is a huge step, but it will be worth the sacrifice. It's one thing to read about orphans or watch a CNN special about them, but nothing compares to the sacred moments you will spend holding and comforting children in need. God will change your life forever when you allow him to take you through the fields of the fatherless.

If you can't leave your own country, you can still step outside of your comfort zone to make a difference. Consider giving five days helping those in your own community who are infected with HIV/AIDS. A fully compassionate response to AIDS must include not only caring for the AIDS orphan, but also the drug user, the gay man, the sex addict, and whomever else comes across our path. As Kay Warren says, "Jesus never asked how someone got sick." We shouldn't either.

STEP 5: GIVE FIVE PEOPLE AN OPPORTUNITY TO JOIN YOU ON YOUR JOURNEY.

You are a force to be reckoned with. Every day, you use the power of word of mouth to encourage or discourage people's behavior. You tell your friends, "Check out this movie," "Don't go to that restaurant," or "You've gotta read this book!" So why not use that same power to get people involved in responding to the AIDS pandemic?

Pastor John Smith of the Concord United Methodist Church in Pennsylvania knows firsthand how this works. He went to Russia with Children's HopeChest, and the orphans he met there changed his life. Since that trip, he's inspired well over a hundred people to get involved just like he did. He's multiplied his influence in amazing ways, and along the way, has helped to change the lives not only of orphans but also of volunteers who've followed in his footsteps. He told me once, "I've brought a few non-Christians over to Russia with me, but I never brought a non-Christian home from a trip." You can spread your influence too.

Here are just a few ideas on how you can do this.

Start a Blog

I have been able to educate and inspire thousands of people to understand God's heart for the orphan through my blog (www.cthomasdavis.com). You can do the same! Blogging is relatively easy and often free. Just visit one of the blogging sites such as TypePad (www.typepad.com), Blogger (www.blogger.com), or

WordPress (www.wordpress.com) and follow the instructions to get started. The great thing about these blog hosting sites is that every time you add a new post, it will immediately be added to the major search engines. So, if you blog about HIV/AIDS and somebody does a search on that subject, your blog will appear in the search. Spread the word, and see how many people you can get excited about helping to solve the HIV/AIDS crisis in Africa.

Tell Everyone You Know

This may seem simple enough, but it only works if you are intentional about it. If you've been on a mission trip, invite your friends to your house for a recap of that trip. Use the time to share your compassion for the people you met and your enthusiasm for the work that's being done. Challenge others to consider how they might help. If you're a member of a small group (a study group, for example), ask if you can lead a session or two focusing on the HIV/AIDS crisis.

Join an Existing Group and Invite Your Friends

Consider joining the One Campaign (www.one.org) or Acting on AIDS (www.worldvision.org/aoa.nsf/aids/home). AOA is a grassroots network of student-led groups committed to creating awareness and being advocates for those impacted by the global AIDS pandemic. After you become a member, invite five of your friends to join too. (And ask them each to invite five of their friends.)

Raise Money with a Charity Badge

There's a lot of complex programming behind a "charity badge," but the idea is simple. Through this service (provided by Network for Good at www.networkforgood.org and Children's HopeChest at www.hopechest.org) you create a "badge," or small informational ad (complete with pictures and text you choose), that you then place on your Web site or blog to raise awareness and money for causes close to your heart. The HTML code is generated for you, and the whole process takes only about five minutes. Once you're done and the badge is up on your site, you can track the donations in real time. Beth Kanter (www.beth.typepad.com) raised over $50,000 for the Sharing Foundation's programs in Cambodia with her charity badge. You'll find lots of great ideas on how to use a charity badge on Katya Andresen's blog, www.nonprofitmarketingblog.com.

Go on a Missions Trip

Whether you're ready to move into the fourth step of the Five for 50 campaign or you just want to head into the missions field as soon as possible, you'll find plenty of worthy organizations ready to help you get started. Here are just a couple.

Children's HopeChest (www.hopechest.org)

The programs of Children's HopeChest connect churches, businesses, and individuals with orphans living around the world. This is the organization I work with, and I lead several trips a year to Russia and Swaziland, two of the locations where we are doing most of our work.

Adventures in Missions (www.adventures.org)

Adventures in Missions organizes and leads mission trips all around the world. Trips range from as short as a week to a year or longer. They take both individuals and groups from age fifteen to adults on age-appropriate trips.

Make a Specific Gift

If you want to give money to a worthy cause, but you're uncomfortable just tossing your dollars into an undesignated fund, consider some of these very specific ways you can contribute to specific needs. You'll find more information on each of these opportunities at www.fivefor50.com.

Feed a hungry child for just fifty cents a day.

Sponsor a "gogo" (a grandmother who cares for orphans). Once you get linked up with one of these rural women, you commit to pray for them and help sell their purses. Selling just four purses a month, or sixty dollars, is equivalent to a part-time job and can help them care for orphans.

Put a child in school. Primary school costs just $100 a year, and secondary school costs only $500 for each child.

Sponsor an orphan party. For just $600 you can give five hundred orphans a rare treat—a feast that includes something they only get once a month—meat—as well as a party that features a night together of spiritual training and fun.

Connect with Compassion International

Compassion International is one of the world's leading mission and child-sponsorship organizations. Their AIDS Initiative is making a real difference in the world. They're leading the way in providing medical treatments, including AIDS-inhibiting antiretroviral therapy (ARVs) and Nevaraprine, a drug that helps to prevent HIV from passing from mother to child. Compassion was one of the first organizations to step up to the plate and respond in such a practical way by making a commitment to providing these much-needed drugs to HIV-positive kids in their sponsorship program *and* their caregivers. Compassion is also offering food, shelter, care, spiritual counseling, and prayer for AIDS orphans.

To join with Compassion in this vital ministry, visit this link on the Web: https://www.compassion.com/contribution/giving/ childvictimsofhiv.htm. You can give a one-time donation or set up a monthly gift. Compassion is quickly becoming one of the leaders in responding to the AIDS crisis, spending tens of millions of dollars to alleviate suffering caused by AIDS.

Change Your Shopping Habits

In our consumer-conscious culture, spending isn't a once-in-a-while luxury, it's more like breathing. While I encourage you to donate directly to those funds that can make the most impact in the lives of those suffering from HIV/AIDS, you can also make a difference simply by "buying different" than you do now. Here are a few ways to do that:

RED Campaign (www.joinred.org)—For every Red product you buy, a portion of the profits goes directly to help fight AIDS in Africa. Companies like Motorola, American Express, Gap, Apple, Giorgio Armani, and Converse are participating.

EDUN (www.edun.ie)—This organization, started by Bono's wife, Ali Hewson, is a clothing company whose mission is to help increase trade and sustainable employment for the developing areas of the world, especially Africa.

Land of a Thousand Hills Coffee (www.landofathousand hillscoffee.com)—This coffee company was started to help subsidize and promote specific projects in Rwanda.

Fair Trade—Here's a way you can make a difference simply by choosing one product over another. When you see the "Fair Trade" logo on an item that means that the farmers who produced the goods were paid a sustainable wage to help support their own families and prevent orphans. Supporting fair trade encourages humanitarian practices around the world. Grounds for Change (www.groundsforchange.org) is my favorite fair trade coffee shop. Pura Vida (www.puravida.com) is also pretty good.

Adopt a Child

If adoption is on your heart, there are many great organizations that can guide you through the process from start to finish. Some organizations will even help you adopt a baby infected with HIV.

American World Adoption Agency (www.awaa.org) sponsors international adoptions in China, El Salvador, Ethiopia, Kazakhstan, Russia, and Ukraine.

Gladney Center for Adoption (www.adoptionsbygladney.com) sponsors domestic and international adoptions in China,

Colombia, Ethiopia, Guatemala, Kazakhstan, Mexico, Russia, Ukraine, and Vietnam.

Bethany Christian Services (www.bethany.org) is the largest national adoption and family service agency in United States. They also assist in international adoption from Albania, China, Colombia, Guatemala, Haiti, Hong Kong, Kazakhstan, Kosovo, Lithuania, Philippines, Russia, South Korea, Ukraine, and Uzbekistan.

Shaohannah's Hope (www.shaohannahshope.com) offers adoption grants and other resources to families seeking to adopt children internationally.

Tapestry Ministry at Irving Bible Church (www.irvingbible.org/index.php?id=759) is a supportive community of adoptive and foster care families that provides adoption-related information and education, support, and encouragement.

The ABBA Fund (www.abbafund.org) offers interest-free loans to those seeking to adopt.

Kingdom Kids Adoption (www.kingdomkidsadoption.org) encourages, educates, and equips adoptive and foster care families.

Investigate Other Resources

We've only scratched the surface of the many amazing and generous organizations that are responding with love and compassion to the AIDS pandemic. In the next section you'll find a long list of other organizations worth investigating. Don't think of this as a boring appendix, as some meaningless list of companies you'll never hear about again. Think of each of them as yet another possible place where you can get involved. This list represents millions of people like you who care enough to make a difference. Learn about these organizations. Then pass the word to others.

THE RED LETTERS LIFE

Here we are, coming to the last pages of the book, but I don't want you to think of this as the end of anything at all. Instead, thing of it as the beginning—the beginning of a Red Letters life. The Red Letters life is a hope-giving life. A life-giving life.

It begins with just one step. You've already taken that step by reading this book. Now it's time to take another step. Before you know it, those steps become a journey. I guarantee this will be the most fantastic journey you've ever been on. It's a journey that can take you across the ocean. A journey that can take you across cultural and economic barriers. A journey you will never forget because of the people you meet. And believe it or not, you'll recognize every one of them.

They look just like Jesus.

ADDITIONAL RESOURCES

Action Against Hunger www.actionagainsthunger.org

Action Against Hunger has been a world leader in the treatment of malnutrition since 1979. It has programs that focus on nutrition, food security, water/sanitation, and basic health in more than forty-four countries around the world.

AERDO www.aerdo.net

The Association of Evangelical Relief and Development Organizations (AERDO) exist to promote excellence in professional practice; to foster networking, collaboration, and information exchange; and enable its membership to effectively support the church in serving the poor and the needy.

American Baptist Churches USA
www.abc-usa.org

American Baptists are a Christ-centered, biblically grounded, ethnically diverse people called to radical personal discipleship in Christ Jesus. Their commitment to Jesus propels them to nurture authentic relationships with one another; build healthy churches; transform their communities, nations, and the world; engage every member in hands-on ministry; and speak the prophetic word in love.

American Jewish World Service www.ajws.org

American Jewish World Service is a not-for-profit international development organization that works on a nonsectarian basis, on behalf of the Jewish community, throughout the developing world and in Russia and Ukraine.

Americans for Informed Democracy
www.aidemocracy.org

Americans for Informed Democracy is a nonpartisan, student-led organization that raises global awareness at more than 250 universities in the United States. They seek to build a global generation that can lead America in our increasingly interdependent world.

Blood:Water Mission www.bloodwatermission.org

Blood and water represent a community-centered and integrated approach to AIDS that include establishing basic conditions necessary for health, addressing the constraints of poverty, and empowering communities to take ownership of their own long-term health development.

Bread for the World Institute www.bread.org/

For more than thirty years, Bread for the World has been a Christian voice for ending hunger. It is a nonpartisan citizens' movement of 54,000 people of faith, including 2,500 churches.

CARE USA www.careusa.org

CARE fights root causes of poverty in the world's poorest communities. They place special focus on working alongside poor women because, equipped with the proper resources, women have the power to help whole families and entire communities escape poverty.

Children's HopeChest www.hopechest.org

Children's HopeChest is responding to God's desire to create a world where every orphan knows Him, experiences family, and acquires the skills necessary for independent life. There are more than 143 million orphaned children in the world and only a very small percentage will experience the blessing of permanent adoption. Through the programs of Children's HopeChest, communities of believers (churches, businesses, ministries, small groups) can engage in direct relationships with orphans in Russia, Eastern Europe, and Africa. Through long-term relationships and professional programs, Children's HopeChest helps thousands of orphans grow into productive, healthy, and faithful adults.

Christian Children's Fund www.christianchildrensfund.org

Christian Children's Fund is creating a better future for more than 7.6 million children and family members in thirty-four countries, helping overcome poverty through education, early childhood development, nutrition, health, livelihood programs, and disaster relief.

Christian Reformed World Relief Committee
www.crwrc.org

CRWRC is a Christian nonprofit organization present in two thousand communities in thirty of the world's poorest countries, where together they are addressing hunger and poverty through emergency disaster assistance, integrated community development programs, and justice education.

Church World Service www.churchworldservice.com

Church World Service, a global humanitarian aid agency and ministry of thirty-six Christian denominations, works to support sustainable self-help and development, meet emergency needs, aid refugees, and address the root causes of poverty and powerlessness.

Citizens for Global Solutions www.globalsolutions.org

Citizens for Global Solutions is a grassroots membership organization that envisions a future in which nations work together to abolish war, protect rights and freedoms, and solve the problems facing humanity that no nation can solve alone.

Compassion International www.compassion.com

Compassion International seeks to release children from poverty in Jesus' name. This is accomplished primarily through Christian child development and child advocacy. Today, their programs encompass much of a child's life—from prenatal care all the way through to leadership development training for qualified young adults. Compassion's AIDS Initiative is a major part of their work in Africa with a four-stage program for alleviating suffering. Through this program, Compassion provides antiretroviral drugs to children and their infected family members and caregivers.

Concern Worldwide (U.S.) Inc.

www.concernusa.org

Founded in 1968, Concern's team of four thousand personnel works in thirty countries providing life-saving emergency relief and long-term assistance (health, education, livelihoods, HIV/AIDS) for the poorest people in the least-developed countries of the world.

CrossRoads www.crossroadslink.org

CrossRoads is a character-based strategy dedicated to helping communities worldwide discover the hope, life, and truth of Jesus Christ in the midst of devastating societal needs such as HIV/AIDS, addictions, and violence.

DATA (debt, AIDS, trade, Africa) www.data.org

DATA aims to spark response to crises threatening hope in Africa: unpayable debts, uncontrolled spread of AIDS, and unfair trade rules that keep Africans poor.

Emergent Village www.emergentvillage.com

Emergent Village is a growing generative friendship among missional Christian leaders seeking to love the world in the Spirit of Jesus Christ.

Engineers Without Borders USA www.ewb-usa.org

EWB-USA partners with developing communities to improve their quality of life through the implementation of environmentally sustainable, equitable, and economical engineering projects while developing internationally responsible engineers and engineering students.

Episcopal Relief and Development www.er-d.org

Episcopal Relief and Development responds to human suffering around the world. They provide emergency assistance after disasters, rebuild communities, and help children and families climb out of poverty.

Evangelical Lutheran Church in America www.elca.org

The 4.9-million-member Evangelical Lutheran Church in America (ELCA) emphasizes worship and prayer, outreach, ecumenical and interfaith dialogue, and preparing professional and lay leaders through college and seminary education.

FORGE www.FORGEnow.org

Facilitating Opportunities for Refugee Growth and Empowerment (FORGE) brings teams of project facilitators to Africa to partner with refugees. By implementing and sustaining projects like HIV/AIDS education, women's empowerment programs, computer centers, and libraries, they create the beginnings of responsible social action by refugees.

A Glimmer of Hope www.aglimmerofhope.org

A Glimmer of Hope is making a sustainable difference in the lives of the rural poor of Ethiopia. By the end of 2005, the foundation had completed more than 1,600 development projects and helped approximately 1.5 million people. It launched its national aid program in Ethiopia in 2001.

Global Health Council www.globalhealth.org

The Global Health Council is the world's largest membership alliance dedicated to saving lives by improving health throughout the world. The council works to ensure that all who strive for improvement and equity in global health have the information and resources they need.

Grameen Foundation USA www.grameenfoundation.org

Grameen Foundation USA is dedicated to reducing global poverty among the poorest of the poor through microfinance. GFUSA partners with fifty-two microfinance institutions in twenty-two countries that provide financial services to empower the poor to start very small businesses to support themselves and their families.

Habitat for Humanity www.habitat.org

Habitat for Humanity is an ecumenical Christian ministry that welcomes to its work all people dedicated to the eradication of poverty housing. Some 200,000 Habitat homes now provide decent, affordable shelter to more than one million people worldwide.

Heartland Alliance www.heartlandalliance.org

Heartland Alliance's mission is to advance the human rights and respond to the human needs of endangered populations through the provision of comprehensive and respectful services and the promotion of permanent solutions leading to a more just global society.

Heifer International www.heifer.org

Heifer envisions a world of communities living together in peace and equitably sharing the resources of a healthy planet. Their mission is to work with communities to end hunger and poverty and to care for the earth.

Hope for Orphans www.familylife.com/hopefororphans

As an outreach of FamilyLife, Hope for Orphans encourages Christians and churches to become involved in orphan ministry. Through various resources and conferences—such as the adoption seminar "If You Were Mine"—Hope for Orphans is helping Christian parents understand and respond to God's heart for orphan ministry.

The Hunger Project www.thp.org

The Hunger Project empowers grassroots people in more than ten thousand villages of Asia, Africa, and Latin America to achieve lasting progress in health, education, nutrition, family incomes, and gender equality.

InterAction www.interaction.org

InterAction is the largest alliance of U.S.-based international development and humanitarian nongovernmental organizations. With more than 160 members operating in every developing country, we work to overcome poverty, exclusion, and suffering by advancing social justice and basic dignity for all.

International Medical Corps www.imcworldwide.org

International Medical Corps is a global, humanitarian, nonprofit organization that saves lives, relieves suffering, and restores self-reliance through health-care training and relief and development programs.

International Rescue Committee www.theirc.org

Founded in 1933, the International Rescue Committee is one of the world's largest nonsectarian, nonprofit organizations providing relief, rehabilitation, protection, and resettlement services for refugees, displaced persons, and victims of oppression

Jubilee USA Network www.jubileeusa.org

Jubilee USA Network is an alliance of seventy-five religious, environmental, human rights, and community groups working for the cancellation of unjust debts to fight poverty in Asia, Africa, and Latin America.

Keep a Child Alive www.keepachildalive.org

Keep a Child Alive is a campaign that offers people the opportunity to provide lifesaving antiretroviral (ARV) medicine and support services directly to children and families with HIV/AIDS in some of the world's poorest countries.

Living Water International www.water.cc

Living Water International (LWI) works in more than twenty-two countries to bring daily access to safe, clean water to over five million people. LWI confronts the global water crisis, as well as hygiene and sanitation development, through a community-based approach of training, consulting, and equipping.

Mennonite Central Committee www.mcc.org

Mennonite Central Committee (MCC) is a relief, service, and peace agency of North American Mennonite and Brethren in Christ churches. MCC seeks to demonstrate God's love by working among people suffering from poverty, conflict, oppression, and natural disaster.

Mercy Corps www.mercycorps.org/home

Mercy Corps is a not-for-profit organization that exists to alleviate suffering, poverty, and oppression by helping people build secure, productive, and just communities.

Millennium Campaign www.millenniumcampaign.org

The Millennium Campaign encourages citizens around the world to hold their governments to account for their promises in the Millennium Declaration and Goals.

National Association of Social Workers www.socialworkers.org

The National Association of Social Workers (NASW) is the largest organization of professional social workers in the world. NASW social workers provide humanitarian assistance for communities in transition, and develop policies to protect human rights both domestically and in international settings.

Nazarene Compassionate Ministries www.ncm.org

Nazarene Compassionate Ministries facilitates projects that address the temporal as well as the spiritual needs of the economically disadvantaged through child development, disaster response, development education, and social transformation.

NetAid www.netaid.org

NetAid educates young people about global poverty and international development, and provides opportunities for them to take concrete actions that make a difference in the lives of the world's poor.

Operation Blessing International www.ob.org

Operation Blessing International (OBI) assists the poor with medical, hunger, and disaster relief. Since 1978, OBI has touched over 179.7 million people in 96 countries and across the U.S. giving goods and services valued at over $943 million.

Opportunity International www.opportunity.org

For 35 years, Opportunity International has fought poverty through small business loans and other financial services. The world's largest Christian microfinance organization, Opportunity serves 810,000 poor entrepreneurs in 27 developing countries.

Our Voices Together www.ourvoicestogether.org

Founded by families and friends who have lost loved ones to terrorist acts, Our Voices Together works to counter terrorism by addressing international poverty and fostering cross-cultural understanding. OVT invites you to join them in building a safer, more compassionate world for all.

Oxfam America www.oxfamamerica.org

Oxfam America helps poor and marginalized communities around the world harness economic opportunities and advocate for their rights (e.g., women's rights, labor rights, indigenous peoples' rights) through grant-making, campaigning, and emergency assistance.

Plan USA www.planusa.org

Plan USA is a global partnership of caring people founded in 1937 to bring hope and help to the world's poorest children. Their community-based programs assist more than ten million children in forty-five developing countries.

RESULTS Educational Fund www.results.org

For twenty-five years, RESULTS Educational Fund has worked to create the political will to end hunger and poverty by training citizens in advocacy, working with the media, and building coalitions in their communities. Through their sister organization, RESULTS, Inc., citizens lobby their own members of congress.

Save Africa's Children www.saveafricaschildren.com

Save Africa's Children (SAC) is among the first and largest African American church organizations providing direct support to AIDS-affected and vulnerable children in Africa. SAC has directly assisted over 350 orphan-care programs in 21 African nations, providing direct support to schools, day-care centers, medical clinics, feeding programs, and children's homes in some of the most remote areas in Africa.

Save the Children www.savethechildren.org

For more than seventy years, Save the Children has created real and lasting change for children in need in more than forty countries around the globe, including the United States.

Sojourners www.sojo.net

Sojourners is a Christian ministry whose mission is to proclaim and practice the biblical call to integrate spiritual renewal and social justice.

UNA-USA www.unausa.org

The United Nations Association of the United States of America (UNA-USA) is the nation's largest grassroots foreign policy organization and the leading center of

UN policy research. UNA-USA offers Americans the chance to connect with key issues like human rights, global health, development, and international justice.

The United Methodist Church www.umc-gbcs.org

The General Board of Church and Society is the public policy and social justice agency of The United Methodist Church. In 2004, the General Conference called for churches in the United States and internationally to work for the achievement of the U.N. Millennium Development Goals.

United Nations Foundation www.unfoundation.org

Founded by Ted Turner, the United Nations Foundation acts to meet the most pressing health, humanitarian, socioeconomic, and environmental challenges, through advocacy, building innovative public-private partnerships, and grant making.

United States Fund for UNICEF www.unicefusa.org

The U.S. Fund for UNICEF supports child survival, protection, and development worldwide through education, advocacy, and fund-raising.

World Concern www.worldconcern.org

World Concern is a Christian humanitarian organization that provides emergency relief and community development in some of the most neglected areas of the world.

World Hope International www.worldhope.org

World Hope International is a faith-based relief and development organization alleviating suffering and injustice through education, enterprise, and community health.

World Hunger Year www.worldhungeryear.org

World Hunger Year (WHY) attacks the root causes of hunger and poverty by promoting effective and innovative community-based solutions that create self-reliance, economic justice, and food security.

World Relief www.wr.org

World Relief is a Christian relief and development organization focused on empowering the church to relieve human suffering, poverty, and hunger worldwide in the name of Jesus Christ.

World Vision www.worldvision.org

World Vision is a Christian relief and development organization dedicated to helping children and their communities worldwide reach their full potential by tackling the causes of poverty.

N O T E S

1. A LIVING GOSPEL

1. *Time*, January 13, 1986.

2. THIS SHRINKING WORLD

1. http://www.thomaslfriedman.com/lexusolivetree.htm.
2. *Boston Globe,* http://www.boston.com/news/politics/conventions/articles/ 2004/07/25/make_aids_a_crucial_topic_at_both_conventions/.
3. G8 Okinawa Summit, Global Poverty Report, July 2000, http://www.worldbank.org/html/extdr/extme/G8_poverty2000.pdf.
4. *The World Factbook,* https://www.cia.gov/cia/publications/factbook/print/xx.html.
5. American Council on Science and Health, http://www.acsh.org/healthissues/newsID.442/healthissue_detail.asp.
6. Henri Nouwen, *Seeds of Hope* (New York: Bantam, 1989), 166–67.

3. THE CRADLE OF CIVILIZATION

1. http://www.bbc.co.uk/worldservice/africa/features/storyofafrica/index_section2.shtml.
2. Nebraska AIDS project, http://www.nap.org/pdf/origin.pdf.
3. Center for Disease Control and Prevention, http://www.cdc.gov/hiv/resources/qa/qa2.htm.
4. AVERT, http://www.avert.org/worlstatinfo.htm.
5. Ibid.
6. World Health Organization (2003), Traditional Medicine, Factsheet No. 134.
7. "Impact African Herbal Medicines on Anti-Retroviral Metabolism," *AIDS Journal* 19, no. 1 (January 3, 2005): 95–97.

4. PANDEMIC

1. The Free Dictionary, http://www.thefreedictionary.com/pandemic.
2. AVERT, http://www.avert.org/worlstatinfo.htm.
3. http://www.themiddleages.net/plague.html.
4. San Francisco Building and Construction Trade Council, http://www.sfbctc.org/21604-middle_class.htm.
5. http://www.theglobeandmail.com/servlet/ArticleNews/TPStory/LAC/20050524/SWAZI24/ TPInternational/Africa.
6. AVERT, http://www.avert.org/safricastats.htm.
7. Testimony of James T. Morris to the Committee on International Relations of the U.S. House of Representatives, http://64.233.167.104/search?q=cache:F7YWwyaeGcYJ:documents.wfp.org/stellent/groups/public/documents/newsroom/wfp076536.pdf+james+t.+morris+hiv+major+role&hl=en&ct=clnk&cd=4&gl=us&client=firefox-a.
8. Southern African Regional Poverty Network, "What is driving the AIDS Epidemic in Swaziland and What Can We Do About It?" http://64.233.167.104/search?q=cache:FEUbcr_pMpYJ:www.sarpn.org.za/documents/d0000706/P786-Whiteside_AIDS_Swaziland_2003.pdf

+http://www.sarpn.org.za/documents/d0000706/P786-Whiteside_
AIDS_Swaziland_2003.pdf&hl=en&ct=clnk&cd=1&gl=us&client=
firefox-a.

9. NPR, http://www.npr.org/templates/story/story.php?storyId=6597207.

10. Harvard University, John F. Kennedy School of Government,
http://www.ksg.harvard.edu/ ksgnews/Features/opeds/062106_
rotberg.htm.

11. DATA, http://www.data.org/whyafrica/issueaids.php.

12. Wikpedia, http://en.wikipedia.org/wiki/World_War_II.

13. The *New York Times*, http://www.nytimes.com/2006/11/22/world/
22aids.html?_r=2&ref=health&oref=slogin&oref=slogin.

14. Ibid.

15. AVERT, http://www.avert.org/ecstatee.htm.

16. Reuters, http://www.alertnet.org/thenews/newsdesk/L17181193.htm.

5. AN INADEQUATE RESPONSE

1. BBC, http://news.bbc.co.uk/2/hi/in_depth/3894733.stm.

2. DATA, http://www.data.org/archives/000605.php.

3. Christian Colligation of Apologetics Debate Research and Evangelism,
http://christiancadre.org/member_contrib/cp_charity.html.

4. Ibid.

5. Alvin Schmidt, *Under the Influence* (Grand Rapids, MI: Zondervan,
2001), 131–32.

6. THE SANCTITY OF LIFE

1. Richard Rohr, *From Wild Man to Wise Man* (Cincinnati: St. Anthony
Messenger Press, 2005), 114–15.

7. A CALL TO JUSTICE

1. American Rhetoric Speech Bank, "Keynote Address at the 54th National Prayer Breakfast," http://www.americanrhetoric.com/speeches/bononationalprayerbreakfast.htm (accessed June 22, 2007).

2. Dr. Joseph D'Souza, "Cry My Beloved Country," http://www.josephdsouza.com/2007/01/cry_my_beloved_country.html.

3. U.S. Constitution Online, http://www.usconstitution.net/dream.html.

4. United Nations, "Fiftieth Anniversary of the Universal Declaration of Human Rights," http://www.un.org/Overview/rights.html (accessed June 22, 2007).

5. Mother Teresa: The Path of Love, "Mother's Wisdom," http://home.comcast.net/~motherteresasite/wis.html (accessed June 22, 2007).

8. THE MOST IMPORTANT THINGS

1. Bono, *ABC Lateline*, http://www.abc.net.au/lateline/content/2006/s1791691.htm.

2. USAID, http://www.usaid.gov/our_work/global_health/aids/News/aidsfaq.html.

3. Abaana, http://www.abaana.org/resources/statistics.cfm.

4. Elie Wiesel Foundation, http://www.eliewieselfoundation.org/ElieWiesel/speech.html.

5. Jeffrey Sachs, *The End of Poverty* (New York: Penguin, 2005), 1.

6. International Atomic Energy Agency, "A Chance for Real Change in Africa," http://www.iaea.org/Publications/Magazines/Bulletin/Bull471/real_change_africa.html (accessed June 22, 2007).

CHILDREN'S HOPECHEST

Since 1994, Children's HopeChest has helped orphans escape a life of poverty, crime, drug abuse, alcoholism, and suicide. Each of our programs connects a caring sponsor—like you—to an orphan in need. You can bring the life-changing grace of Jesus Christ to an orphan. You can give them the confidence to face an unfriendly world—and a safe place to find friends and mentors.

Get Involved. Join the Five for 50 Campaign.

Children's HopeChest is proud to participate in the *Five for 50* campaign—five practical ways to make a positive impact in the lives of nearly 50 million people suffering from AIDS worldwide. Here are several ways you can get involved today:

1. **Take the next step.** Visit us at www.hopechest.org to find out more about how you can care for orphans through the programs of Children's HopeChest.

2. **Start giving today.** Go to www.Fivefor50.com and make your pledge to help orphans in Russia or Swaziland. You can make a difference for as little as $5/month.

3. **Come with us on a trip.** Contact Children's HopeChest at 1-800-648-9575 about joining us on Tom's next vision trip. Put what you've learned here into action by being Christ's hands and feet.

God hears the cry
of the orphan…
…how will you respond?

THE CAMPAIGN TO MAKE POVERTY HISTORY
WWW.ONE.ORG

There is a plague of biblical proportions taking place in Africa right now, but we can beat this crisis, if we each do our part. The first step is signing the ONE Declaration to join the ONE Campaign.

The ONE Campaign is a new effort to rally Americans, ONE by ONE, to fight the emergency of global AIDS and extreme poverty. We are engaging Americans everywhere we gather– in churches and synagogues, on the internet and college campuses, at community meetings and concerts.

Together, we can all make a difference in the lives of the poorest of God's children.

We invite you to join the ONE Campaign.

"The true state of emergency lies within the church—it lies within us. It's our problem. We can't leave Africa's children lying by the side of the road as we pass on by."
----*Tom Davis*

To learn more about ONE, please visit **WWW.ONE.ORG.**

ONE Voice can make a difference.

Join the ONE Campaign now!